BIRD WALKS

IN

RHODE ISLAND

BIRD WALKS

IN

RHODE ISLAND

Exploring the Ocean State's Best Sanctuaries

ADAM J. FRY

Illustrations by Keith Gannon

Backcountry Publications
Woodstock, Vermont

An invitation to the reader

Over time trails and roads can be rerouted and signs and landmarks altered. If you find that changes have occurred in the sanctuaries described in this book, please let us know so that corrections can be made in future editions. The author and publisher also welcome other comments and suggestions. Address all correspondence to:

Editor, Bird Walks
Backcountry Publications
P.O. Box 175
Woodstock, Vermont 05091

Library of Congress Cataloging-in-Publication Data

Fry, Adam J., 1966–
    Bird walks in Rhode Island: rambles through the ocean state's
best sanctuaries / Adam J. Fry; illustrations by Keith Gannon.
        p.   cm.
    Includes bibliographical references and index.
    ISBN 0-88150-218-9
    1. Bird watching—Rhode Island—Guide-books.   2. Wildlife
refuges—Rhode Island—Guide-books.   3. Rhode Island—
Description and travel—1981– —Guide-books.   I. Title.
    QL684.R4F79   1992
    598'.07234745—dc20   91-38240
                                                                  C I P

Published by Backcountry Publications
A Division of the Countryman Press, Inc.
Woodstock, Vermont 05091
Printed in the United States of America by BookCrafters on acid-free, recycled paper.

Cover and text design by Ann Aspell
Maps by Dick Widhu
Photo on page 124 by Noble Proctor; all other photos by the author

10   9   8   7   6   5   4   3   2   1

To Noble Proctor and Grit Ardwin,
the two best friends a birder could have!

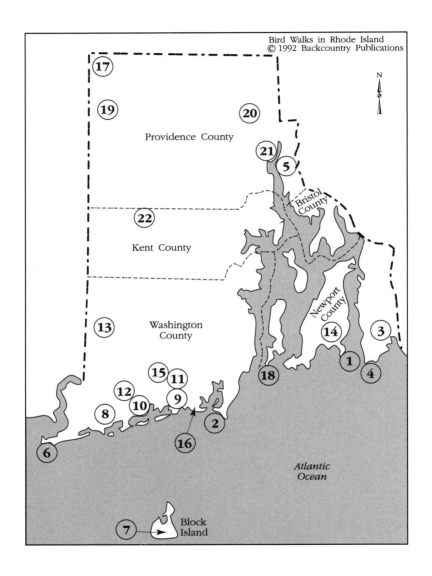

Bird Walks in Rhode Island
© 1992 Backcountry Publications

N

17

19

20

Providence County

21

5

Bristol County

22

Kent County

Newport County

13

Washington County

14

3

1

15 11

4

12

18

10

9

8

2

6

16

Atlantic Ocean

7 → Block Island

Contents

▼

Acknowledgments

I would like to thank a few people who gave considerable support in the preparation of this manuscript. Hugh Willoughby and Ruth Doan MacDougall lent their editing skills to improve earlier and final drafts. To Paula Spirito I am deeply indebted for typing and retyping numerous versions. Credit for the initial mapwork goes to Gil George, who may be the busiest man I know but still found time to prepare them. And, finally, I would like to thank Keith Gannon for the wonderful artwork.

.

Introduction

▼

In this smallest state in the Union, almost 400 species of birds have been recorded, 160 of which can be found breeding within its borders yearly. Since there are probably several private ranches in Texas larger than Rhode Island, these numbers are remarkable and suggest the rewards of bird-watching here.

The many advantages of birding in such a tiny state include short travel distances. You can reach any point, coastal or inland, usually in less than an hour, and thus if you learn of the appearance of a rare bird which might or might not stay, you can get to it before it leaves. And because Rhode Island is close to several other good birding states (Massachusetts and Connecticut, for example), if birds of interest show up there it doesn't take long to go see them; you can enjoy good birding in several states at the same time.

Also, in such a small state you tend to know all of the active birders, so a good communication network can be established.

Rhode Island is fortunate to have approximately 400 miles of coastline. As with most coastal states, however, public access to the shores is often severely limited by private ownership. The coastal areas listed in this book are among the few places where you can walk the shore without worrying about trespassing on somebody's property. Along the coast and elsewhere, many of the birding areas are wonderfully scenic places to hike as well as to bird-watch.

HOW TO USE THIS BOOK

This book is intended as a guide and aid for residents and visitors, for experienced bird-watchers and novices—and for those who simply enjoy observing nature as they walk.

Seasons. After the title of each area, you will see the abbreviations "S." for spring, "Su." for summer, "F." for fall, and "W." for winter. These symbols are followed by one, two, or three stars, which indicate the best season to visit the area. One star means fair birding, two stars mean good birding, and three stars mean great birding.

The spring migration peaks during the first two weeks in May. The fall migration begins in late July and usually lasts well into November. As in other states, Rhode Island's birding in mid-summer or mid-winter is much less exciting than during the spring and fall migrations, but in summer we do have some interesting breeding birds, including Northern Harriers, Grasshopper Sparrows, Red-breasted Nuthatches, and a tremendous number of Wood Ducks.

Although Rhode Island cannot claim to have such sought-after species as Texas and Arizona do with Colima Warbler and Elegant Trogan, respectively, the one claim to fame we have is that the largest populations of wintering Harlequin Ducks on the East Coast are found at Sachuest Point in Middletown.

And the state is the winter home to a large number of sea ducks, including Red-breasted Mergansers, Buffleheads, scoters, and scaups, as well as other species such as Horned and Red-necked Grebes and Common and Red-throated Loons. (Be advised: Winter birding at the coast in Rhode Island is very cold. Dress warmly and bring plenty of food along.)

For hikers, late spring and late fall are by far the best times to visit. May and October are probably the most enjoyable months for walking; temperatures are mild, insect activity is minimal, and you will usually find an abundance of early-flowering or late-flowering plants.

Travel. At the start of each chapter are directions to the particular area discussed. Although Rhode Island is the second most densely populated state (after New Jersey), it is an easy state to travel in.

The major roads frequently used in this book are I-95 which runs the length of the state from Connecticut to Massachusetts, RI 138 over the Newport Bridge which for many is the quickest way to get to Newport and Middletown (home to events such as the Newport Jazz Festival and, formerly, the America's Cup races), I-195 east which takes you from Providence, Rhode Island, to Cape Cod, Massachusetts, and US 1 along the south shore which is the best way to reach many important coastal parks and wildlife refuges.

Birds. The main part of each chapter is devoted to information about what species to look for. I realize that some of the accounts of species in particular areas may seem exaggerated, but my aim is to list what species have been seen in the past in order to give you an idea of the types of sightings that are possible. All species listed for a particular area, unless otherwise indicated, have been seen at the location either by me or by other birders, recently or historically.

I have not included *all* good birding areas in the state. I have omitted some because the habitats could not withstand frequent visitors. In other cases, the only access is through private property; if you want to visit these areas, try speaking to the landowners. You will probably find, as I have, that most are willing to allow you to cross their property and that many are very interested in what you find.

In the index are listed all the species mentioned in the text, and their locations. Use the index to direct you to the locations of birds you particularly want to see. Also use it for finding the locations of birding areas that local birders may suggest to you or that you may hear on the Rare Bird Alert tape.

This Rare Bird Alert is sponsored by the Audubon Society of Rhode Island. Most states have such a Rare Bird Alert phone number, which local and visiting birders can call to learn what types of rare or interesting birds have been seen in an area recently. These phone numbers are particularly helpful because they let you know if a bird you have seen has also been seen across the state. In Rhode Island, when you call you will usually hear about the common birds in the state, but occasionally a rare bird actually makes it onto the Alert. The number is (401) 231-5728. To report a rare bird, call the Audubon Society at (401) 231-6444.

SUGGESTIONS FOR NOVICE BIRD-WATCHERS

Bird-watching is one of the most enjoyable ways to spend time outdoors. It can be done casually as you take a walk, or you can make it the reason for a walk, going to an area specifically to see a special bird.

Because beginners find it difficult at times to identify birds, binoculars and a field guide are essential. A good pair of lightweight binoculars are 7x35 binoculars, which provide clear images with a manageable level of magnification. Most importantly, they are reasonably priced, usually less than $150. Start with the lowest priced models; do not spend a lot of money only to discover that you don't have time to use them! (In addition to bird-watching, 7x35 binoculars are useful for boating, shows, etc., and when inverted they act as a magnifying glass.)

After a while, you may want to invest in a spotting scope, a telescope used for bird-watching. Spotting scopes are considerably more powerful than binoculars and therefore allow you to see birds that are very far away, such as most sea ducks. They are particularly useful in the wintertime when most interesting birds are typically far from shore, but they are almost useless in the woodlands because they are so powerful you cannot usually focus close enough to see the birds.

The best field guide for beginning birders on the East Coast is Roger Tory Peterson's *Field Guide to the Birds East of the Rockies*. Color plates accompany the species descriptions. The nice thing about this guide is that most of the western birds that we rarely—if ever—see in the East are omitted, reducing confusion.

Equipped with binoculars and field guide, look carefully at the birds, noting as many aspects of their plumage as you can, as well as their habitats and behavior.

Do not be frustrated. Bird-watching is intended for fun— if it isn't, you are doing something wrong! It takes years of field experience to identify confidently and accurately all the birds you see, so don't be embarrassed if you cannot identify every bird right away.

Talk to other birders you meet in the field. You will soon learn that, in general, birders are a friendly lot. Most will gladly assist in identifying a troublesome species. And only by listening to other birders can you learn the innumerable tricks for identifying common and uncommon species that the most popular field guides never seem to tell you.

Spend as much time in the field as you can. How good a birder you will be is determined by the amount of time you spend birding. Remember, however, that good birders do not look down on people who spend less time than they do birding; in fact, good birders probably enjoy the company of those who know slightly less of the sport—it gives them a chance to show off a bit.

You may want to begin keeping a life list, a list of all the birds you see in your lifetime. There are many different types of life lists. For example, you can keep what is called a state list, which is a life list of all the bird species you see within a particular state's borders. Many people even keep year lists in which they record the bird species seen during the year, to compare with past or future years. The most common type of list is the North American life list, in which you record the number of species seen on the continent of North America, the boundaries of which are defined by the American Birding Association.

You may also want to participate in Christmas Bird Counts. Sponsored by the National Audubon Society, these are annual counts of birds in a given area during a given time period, usually from about two weeks before Christmas to the first week of the new year. Counts were originally established to try to see long-term trends in species numbers. Results of

Christmas Bird Counts are published in *American Birds* magazine, so if you wish to know what birds were wintering in a locality anywhere in the country you simply look it up in the magazine. Examples of counts in Rhode Island are the Block Island count, the South County count, and the Newport County count. For more information on counts, call your local Audubon Society.

1

Sachuest Point National Wildlife Refuge

▼

Specialties: Sea Ducks

S.*, Su.*, F.**, W.***

▼

Sachuest Point National Wildlife Refuge is a wonderful oceanside refuge located at the extreme southeastern tip of Middletown. Lying adjacent to long stretches of beachfront, it consists of a big rock-lined peninsula jutting into Rhode Island Sound and is sheltered on the west by Newport and on the east by Little Compton. These sheltering landmasses on either side produce a relatively calm-watered area fit for large concentrations of wintering sea ducks.

Many other interesting species can be found here. Migrant hawks, including the scarce Peregrine Falcon and Merlin, and wintering raptors such as the Snowy Owl and Rough-legged Hawk, are seen intermittently almost every winter.

You should be warned, however, that winter birding at Sachuest can often be extremely cold, so to enjoy this walk it is wise to dress very warmly.

Another warning: This area is completely overrun with tourists and beach-goers during the summer. Fortunately, it is the winter birds which are the feature here!

DIRECTIONS

From the north, take RI 138 (East Main Road) south to RI 138A (Aquidneck Avenue). Follow that road south until you

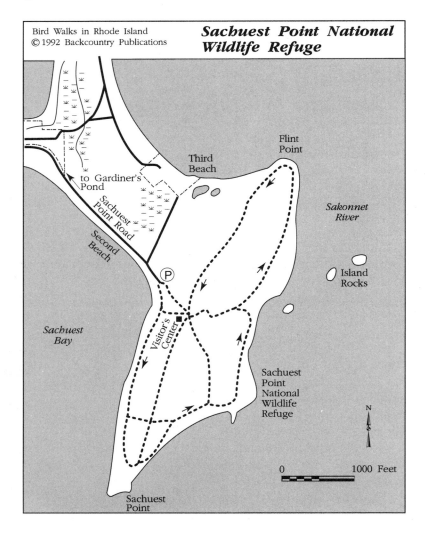

Bird Walks in Rhode Island
© 1992 Backcountry Publications

*Sachuest Point National
Wildlife Refuge*

come to the Atlantic Ocean. Turn left onto Sachuest Point
Road and drive to the refuge parking lot at its end.

From the west, take RI 138 over the Newport Bridge. Take
the "Downtown Newport" exit, turning right onto RI 238
south. Drive .3 mile to the second traffic light, and then turn

right toward the Newport Visitors' Information Center. Follow this main thoroughfare through seven traffic lights. At one of the intersections you will have to bear left, but in general you will keep heading east toward the beaches. As Memorial Boulevard starts down a long hill, you will see Easton's Beach (locally "First Beach") on your right. Keep going straight ahead as you enter Middletown at the east end of the beach. In another couple of miles Sachuest Beach ("Second Beach") will appear on the right. Continue east on Sachuest Point Road to its end at the refuge parking lot.

At the Sachuest Point National Wildlife Refuge, the Visitors' Center is open only on holidays and weekends from 8:00 A.M. to 4:00 P.M., but when open can provide you with a wealth of information (small exhibit hall, brochures, maps), as well as modern rest rooms.

BIRDING

As you walk from the parking lot to the Visitors' Center (150 feet), be alert for foraging Short-eared Owls and Northern Harriers (winter only) as they work the grassy areas in search of the abundant Meadow Voles which form the base of the raptor food chain here. The harriers are easily detected as they tilt and glide low over the grasslands.

The best place to start your serious birding, though, is back at the beach along Sachuest Point Road, which skirts the end of Sachuest Bay. If you walk back from your parking spot to the beach, you can pick up the unmarked trail that goes around the entire refuge. Here at the beginning of your hike, gulls of various sorts can be studied at close range, and Sanderlings can often be found scampering along the sandy beach (winter), together with Dunlins which will usually be too busy foraging through the seaweed at the high-tide mark to pay any attention to you.

As you start walking south along the abandoned dirt road which here is actually the hiking trail, be sure to scan the bay at your right very carefully; because of its protective waters, it often shelters some of the specialties of this area. Look for Oldsquaw, an attractive sea duck found here regularly after the first of November—usually in small numbers, however. Some of the other species seen well in this sheltered bay, although they may also be found on the ocean side, are Common Goldeneye, Bufflehead, Common Loon (up to 20), Horned Grebe, White-winged Scoter, and both Greater and (rarely) Lesser Scaups. Other birds that seem to prefer this side of the refuge are Red-throated Loons, and Red-necked Grebes (Sachuest is the best place in the state to find this species); they are never seen as often as Common Loons or Horned Grebes, but in some years can be easy to find. Another species of particular interest is Barrow's Goldeneye. At least one adult drake has been a regular winter visitor for many years. By carefully looking with your spotting scope, you probably will turn him up among the large flocks of Common Goldeneyes (usually females) after the first week of December.

Continue walking south along the bay for about .7 mile to Sachuest Point itself. Along the way many wintering sparrows will make their presence known by their chip notes. The thin "seet" of the Savannah Sparrow can easily be heard; with practice it can be readily separated from the similar call note of the White-throated Sparrow, which is also a common winter visitor to the refuge. Other wintering sparrows that you are likely to see include Tree, Song, Field, and possibly White-crowned. If you are really lucky, you may catch a glimpse of a Clay-colored or a Lark Sparrow, each of which invariably shows up somewhere along the Rhode Island coast during the fall migration and early winter. In addition, many late migrant or even wintering songbirds are attracted to the coastal thickets of Bayberry and Honeysuckle, so swatting the brush for stragglers such as Gray Catbird, Brown Thrasher, and Rufous-sided Towhee can often be productive.

As you reach the point, walk slowly because Snow Buntings are rather regular here (late fall and early spring). If you do see a small flock of these coastal wanderers, check it closely for the much darker Lapland Longspurs which are occasionally found with the buntings. The rocks at the point are excellent for Purple Sandpipers, and half a mile out to sea Cormorant Rock almost always lives up to its name. In winter, it often harbors a couple of hundred Great Cormorants. While you scan the rock, look also for Bonaparte's Gulls and—after easterly storms—for pelagic (oceanic) species such as Black-legged Kittiwakes. And at the height of the Northern Gannet migration (early November to early December), these huge birds are easy to locate; just look for their long, black-tipped white wings as they plunge menacingly into the cold ocean far offshore. A few Northern Gannets may occur throughout the winter.

After you round the point and head northward, your next important stop will be the Island Rocks (.4 mile), for it is here that the spectacular little sea ducks for which this refuge is best known can be found. If you search among the roughest swells of water around these rocky islets, you should be able to see small concentrations of Harlequin Ducks. These beautiful ducks first appear in Rhode Island waters during the first week of November; they often stay well into March. Their numbers have slowly built up for the last decade or so, and it is not unusual now to find as many as 60 of them—the best viewing

Harlequin Duck

in the Northeast of these colorful northern visitors. Although you may spot them sunning themselves on the rocks amid the foraging Purple Sandpipers, your best bet is to examine the roughest, most turbulent water, for it is in such places of violence that the Harlequin seems to thrive. Another particularly beautiful duck is the Common Eider, which seems to enjoy sunbathing even more than the Harlequin Ducks and can frequently be seen sitting on the rocks secure above the battering waves. One or two of the Common Eider's northern cousin, the King Eider, will put in an appearance here each winter but usually will make an exit after only a few days, whereas the Common Eiders may stay for weeks at a time.

Just past Island Rocks you can usually see large flocks of scoters floating in "rafts" (the term that describes groups of waterfowl resting on the water). Often all three species are present in winter, although they do not occur in equal numbers. The White-winged is the most common of the scoters here, with males and the more drab females making up the bulk of the rafts. The Surf Scoter runs a somewhat close second; the males can easily be picked out even at a considerable distance, as their gaudy orange-and-white head markings are highly conspicuous. The Black Scoter is, however, another story. This species can often blend in very inconspicuously with the other scoters. To make matters worse, it also seems to vary greatly in daily abundance; one day you may be able to spot a hundred or more of them while the next day you may be lucky to find even one.

After checking the rafts of scoters and scaups, continue walking north along the trail to Flint Point (.5 mile). There you will note a small observation tower which offers a fine view of the Sakonnet Passage of Narragansett Bay. As you look out over the water, be sure to listen in the thickets behind you for Ring-necked Pheasants; the loud squawking of the males is very distinctive as they rustle through the underbrush. Continue south along the main trail toward the Visitors' Center, remembering to keep your eyes on the fields and thickets for Northern Harriers, Short-eared Owls, American Kestrels,

Eastern Meadowlarks, Northern Flickers, and red foxes. You may even find something unusual, such as the Common Redpolls which showed up here during one recent Christmas Bird Count.

You have completed your tour of Sachuest Point National Wildlife Refuge, but before you leave the area you will want to check a nearby spot, Gardiner's Pond. This reservoir is located approximately 1 mile away from the refuge parking lot and is easily reached by taking the second right as you head back (west) along Sachuest Point Road. One hundred feet after you turn north, park in the small dirt clearing on your right. Cross the plank bridge over the stream and climb the 30-foot dike to the pond. This reservoir can be one of the better places in the state to view migrating waterfowl at a reasonably close range. On some of the warmer days in October and November, as many as fifteen species can be seen here, usually including all three species of merganser, Greater and Lesser Scaups, Ruddy Duck, American Wigeon, Mallard, American Black Duck, Canvasback, Redhead (rare), Canada Goose, American Coot, and occasionally Snow Goose (both blue and white phases). Occasionally Pied-billed Grebes can be studied here as well.

2

Point Judith and Galilee

▼

Specialties: Gulls and Wintering Birds

S.**, Su.*, F.**, W.***

▼

If you are looking for a birding area that can afford you the best chance for finding rare gulls or alcids in the state of Rhode Island, make a trip to Point Judith and Galilee.

There are several sandy beaches along this loop where you can often find large numbers of roosting gulls, a large saltwater marsh where shorebirds often congregate, and, jutting out into Block Island Sound, an unsheltered peninsula called Point Judith Light which is by far the prime area in the state to find wintering alcids.

DIRECTIONS

From the north, follow I-95 south from Providence for 13.5 miles to RI 4 south, Exit 9, "North Kingstown." RI 4 south becomes US 1 south after about 6.5 miles. Follow US 1 south for approximately 11 miles to the Point Judith exit, "Point Judith, Scarborough," and proceed off this exit to the first traffic light. Turn right at this light and follow RI 108 south to the Fishermen's Memorial State Park (3.6 miles).

From the west, Exit 1 off I-95 will put you on RI 3 south. Follow RI 3 south until it intersects with RI 216 (1.7 miles), and continue on RI 216 south for approximately 6.4 miles to US 1, which runs the length of what Rhode Islanders call the South Shore. After turning left onto US 1 north, follow this road for 14.5 miles to the "Narragansett, Point Judith" exit.

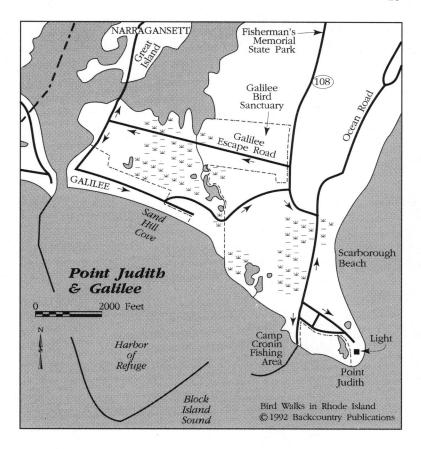

Turn right at the end of this exit for .5 mile to a traffic light. Turn right here and proceed as above.

BIRDING

The first stop on this birding loop is Fishermen's Memorial State Park. After turning into the park, drive straight ahead to the gate (locked except during the summer months) and park here. There are several trails that will take you through typical coastal thickets which can often harbor some interesting species, especially during migration. Often I have seen migrant flocks of warblers and thrushes hiding in the thickets on an early morning in May or October, and this park can frequently also harbor large flocks of swallows, particularly Tree Swallows which seem to favor the large Bittersweet tangles during migration.

Winter birding can be productive as well. Often there are great numbers of Yellow-rumped Warblers that winter here along with the occasional Gray Catbirds and Hermit Thrushes that attempt to stay the winter. In fact, even a Northern Waterthrush was found here during a recent Christmas Bird Count.

Because of the large summer crowds that gather here, the best birding at this park is confined to the winter and fall migrations—especially the months of October, November, December, and January.

The next birding location on this loop is the marsh off Galilee Escape Road. To reach this road continue south on RI 108 for 1 mile to a traffic light. Turn right onto Galilee Escape Road and follow it until you see the marsh on your right (1 mile). This marsh is often used by clam diggers during the warmer months, but pay no attention to them because the migrant shorebirds do not seem to mind.

Interesting fall shorebirds are the focus of this area—Stilt Sandpiper, Long-billed Dowitcher, and even Whimbrel have been seen here. These are, however, the uncommon ones. Other shorebirds that occur more commonly are Greater and Lesser Yellowlegs, Black-bellied Plover, Short-billed Dowitcher, and Semipalmated Plover (often the most abundant bird on the exposed mud flats), and the months of September and October have in the past produced marsh birds such as Clapper Rail and America Bittern. If you are really lucky you may even flush a King Rail; the first week in October is the best time to attempt this feat.

As the cool days of fall become the cold days of winter, waterfowl can often be found gathering on the open water at this marsh. Common species include Black Ducks, Buffleheads (very common in January), and Canada Geese, as well

*Peregrine
Falcon*

as small flocks of wintering shorebirds, Dunlins and Sander-lings, which can usually be seen wandering around the muddy shoreline. If you are feeling particularly daring on the day you visit this marsh, you may wish to put on a pair of high boots and walk through the marsh to try to scare up a Common Snipe or a Clapper Rail. In fact, by doing this, other birders have found wintering Sharp-tailed Sparrows here.

Shorebirds as a group breed much farther north than the limits of this small state extend; thus, they only pass through during the spring and fall migrations, and as a result the best birding at this coastal marsh is done during the few months in the spring and fall when they are either moving northward to breed or southward to their winter quarters.

Another spot to check for shorebirds is Little Comfort Island (locally Great Island). To reach this island, continue west on Galilee Escape Road to Great Island Road (.5 mile). Turn right onto this road, and after crossing the bridge turn left onto the first road, which will lead you around the perim-eter of the island and back to Great Island Road.

At low tide, the mud flats surrounding the island can often harbor flocks of shorebirds. Ruddy Turnstones, Least and Semipalmated Sandpipers, and Short-billed Dowitchers can be found here in the fall. These migrants are often joined by flocks of Brants and Laughing Gulls that can be seen foraging in the shallow water at the edge of the flats.

Winter birding here may also produce some interesting species. The boat piers should be checked for Glaucous and

Iceland Gulls (uncommon) as well as Bonaparte's Gulls (common winter visitor). This area is also one of the best places in the state to find wintering Pied-billed Grebes, Black-bellied Plovers, and Killdeers.

After completing this loop and returning to Great Island Road, continue south on this road, over the bridge, to the Galilee Fishing Area (recently renamed Salty Brine State Beach), 1 mile. The parking lot at the Galilee Fishing Area simply provides a different angle from which to search the piers for interesting gulls. Glaucous, Iceland, and Bonaparte's Gulls can be found with regularity (winter only), and even Common Black-headed, Little, and Lesser Black-backed Gulls have been seen here. In fact, even a young Thayer's Gull was found here during one winter.

Roger W. Wheeler Memorial Beach (locally Sand Hill Cove) is the next spot to check for birds, particularly in late fall and winter when the large summer crowds have dispersed. After leaving the Galilee Fishing Area parking lot, turn right onto Sand Hill Cove Road. Follow this road east for .6 mile to the Roger W. Wheeler Memorial Beach parking area. Park near the pavilion, which offers the best vantage point for birding.

Common Loon, Common Goldeneye, Surf and White-winged Scoters, and Horned Grebe are fairly common just offshore during the winter months. Oldsquaw—a somewhat uncommon wintering sea duck along the Rhode Island coast—can usually be found at this beach in small numbers, particularly between the months of November and March. Look for their generally whitish plumage and the long, needle-shaped tail that often points straight up into the air. Wheeler Beach is the one place that I would recommend if you wish to add Oldsquaw to your Rhode Island list.

During the fall migration, the beach edge should be scanned for American Pipits, Horned Larks, and Lapland Longspurs with the small flocks of Snow Buntings that can occasionally be found here.

After birding this beach, continue east on Sand Hill Cove Road for approximately 1.5 miles to its end (RI 108 intersection). Turn right onto RI 108 south until you come to a four-way stop. At the stop turn right, and bearing left follow this road until you reach the lighthouse (2 miles).

The pond at the lighthouse can often harbor migrant egrets and herons and an occasional Solitary Sandpiper. In the winter, however, the only birds you will see are a small group of Gadwall that appears fairly regularly when the pond is not frozen. If the pond is frozen, you should move on to the next stop: Camp Cronin Fishing Area.

You can reach the fishing area by heading back up the lighthouse road for approximately .1 mile to a dirt road on your left. Follow this road to a small parking area by the shore. You have now reached one of the best coastal birding spots in the state. Once again, because of the summer crowds, winter birding is the only option for birders.

Looking west over Point Judith lighthouse pond

The best way to bird this area is to direct your binoculars or spotting scope out over the water and see what you can find. Many good species have been recorded from this point. Terns are often found here. Least Terns, Roseate Terns (becoming more difficult to find), and Common Terns are the ones seen during the summer months, but migrants are the attraction for most birders at this park.

During migration—especially late fall—Peregrine Falcons, Black Terns, Forster's Terns (becoming easier to find), and an occasional Black Skimmer can sometimes be seen. If you can get to the point early in the morning after a big storm, you may be lucky enough to see species such as Bridled Tern, Sooty Tern, or Sandwich Tern, much as the birders did who came down after the hurricanes of 1979 and 1991.

December, January, and February are the best months to look for alcids. Most alcids are very difficult to identify on the water, and are very rare in Rhode Island, but if you pay close attention to key field marks, you may be able to identify a Razorbill, Thick-billed Murre, Dovekie, or Black Guillemot. Other distant seabirds that you may see include Northern Gannet, Black-legged Kittiwake, Manx Shearwater (spring), and even Pomarine and Parasitic Jaegers (generally in the fall).

Point Judith is also a good spot from which to see the usual winter specialties such as White-winged Scoters, Red-throated Loons, Red-necked Grebes, and Red-breasted Mergansers.

The last stop along the Point Judith and Galilee loop is Scarborough State Beach. To reach this beach drive back to the four-way stop and proceed straight (north) on Ocean Road for 1.5 miles to the Scarborough State Beach parking area.

Red-breasted Mergansers, Common Loons, and Horned Grebes are common winter visitors as well as Great Cormorants, but instead of winter birding the activity that I find most enjoyable here is listening to fall migrants as they pass overhead. The best time to do this is on a cool autumn night when the sky is clear and the beach is empty. The sounds of many migrants can be heard as they fly over the point; their calls and chip notes seem almost continuous as these small birds try to maintain contact with their flocks on the long journey south. Many species which migrate at night give characteristic flight calls. While many of these calls will sound similar at first, with practice you may be able to differentiate between the sharp "spee-ahh" of the Gray-cheeked Thrush (first week in October) and the lower-pitched, less emphatic "shurk" or "pweep" of the Veery (first week in September). Good luck!

3

Quicksand Pond

▼

Specialties: Shorebirds, Egrets

S.***, Su.**, F.***, W.*

▼

Quicksand Pond is a large tidally influenced pond located at the southeastern tip of Little Compton and, in fact, forms part of the boundary between Rhode Island and Massachusetts. Because of the large mud flats that are often exposed at this pond, considerable numbers of shorebirds gather here to feed during the spring and fall migrations. Unfortunately, the breachway (sluiceway) that allows water to leave the pond is unpredictable and may or may not be open when you visit. If it has been recently opened, the large expanses of fresh, wet mud will attract almost all of the shorebird species regular in Rhode Island. It is for this reason that Quicksand Pond is one of the best shorebirding areas in the state as well as a prime location to look for rare or uncommon species.

DIRECTIONS:

From the north, follow I-195 east from Providence to Massachusetts Exit 8A, "Tiverton, RI / Newport, RI" (approximately 20 miles). Proceed south on this road (RI 24) to the second Tiverton exit ("Fish Road, Tiverton") and turn left at the end of the exit. Follow this road south for 1.4 miles until you reach the RI 177 intersection—turn right here and proceed for 2 miles to RI 77. Turn left (south) onto RI 77 and follow this road for 7.5 miles to Peckham's Greenhouse on your left. At the greenhouse turn left and continue for 1 mile

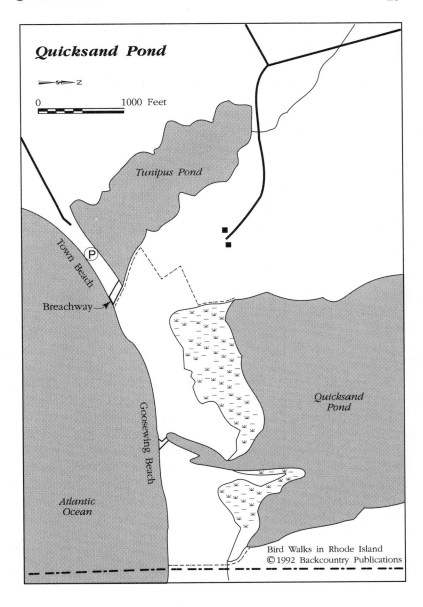

Quicksand Pond

0   1000 Feet

Tunipus Pond

Town Beach

P

Breachway

Quicksand
Pond

Goosewing Beach

Atlantic
Ocean

Bird Walks in Rhode Island
©1992 Backcountry Publications

until you reach a stop sign. Turn right here and follow this road to its end (1 mile). Turn right and proceed for .5 mile to Sneeker's Restaurant; 500 feet after the restaurant, the road will turn sharply right—you should turn left here. After 1 mile this road will also turn right; you will need to make a quick left turn just after the curve. Follow this road to the Town Beach parking area and park on the far side of the lot. There is a fee charged for parking at this beach during the summer. Fortunately, however, the summer birds are not the main birding attraction.

From the west, take RI 138 over the Newport Bridge (toll $2). Continue on RI 138 north for 10.7 miles until you reach RI 24 north. Follow RI 24 north to the first Tiverton exit ("Tiverton, Little Compton; RI 77 to RI 177"). After reaching RI 77 south follow the above directions from I-195 east.

BIRDING:

Before you reach Quicksand Pond there are a few good stops along RI 77 south. Seapowet Marshes and the Emilie Ruecker Wildlife Refuge are the first. You can reach this area by following RI 77 south for 1.8 miles past the RI 177 intersection. Turn right onto Seapowet Avenue and continue on this road for .5 mile to the Ruecker parking area. Ruecker encompasses a large salt marsh that can be productive for waders, shorebirds, and other marsh birds, such as Northern Harriers and wintering waterfowl. You can reach the Seapowet Marshes by continuing west on Seapowet Avenue to the large saltwater marsh on your left (1 mile). Glossy Ibis, Little Blue Heron, and Snowy Egret frequent this area during the summer; even Tricolored Herons are seen here regularly (early spring and fall).

Approximately 1 mile from Seapowet Avenue, there is a large field on your left, one of the better spots in Rhode Island to see Cattle Egrets. You will also see Barn and Tree Swallows hunting low over the grass. Finally, a small pond will appear on your left (approximately .8 mile south of the Cattle Egret

*Long-Billed
Dowitcher*

field). This pond is a watering hole for cattle; therefore, the soft mud constantly churned by these cattle provides excellent feeding opportunities for Common Snipe and American Woodcock. Also, Solitary Sandpipers are occasionally found at the pond's edge during the spring and fall migrations.

Continue on to the main section of this loop. After you park at Town Beach, you should look directly north (behind the parking area) and into Tunipus Pond. Migrating and wintering waterfowl are often abundant on this pond—species of particular interest include Redhead (uncommon), Ring-necked Duck, Lesser Scaup, Green-winged and (rarely) Blue-winged Teals, and Canvasback. Indeed, nearly all of the migrating and wintering ducks that occur in our area may be found on this pond at the right time. On the ocean side a quick look for sea ducks can often be productive; Common Golden-eye and Bufflehead are the regular winter visitors. Bonaparte's Gulls are sometimes seen here during the winter, so look for them dipping and plunging for food close to the shore.

Proceed on foot east across the Tunipus Pond breach-

way—there is usually a large plank to make crossing easier—
to Quicksand Pond. Quicksand Pond is most notable for the
large concentrations of shorebirds that gather here during the
spring and fall migrations. Black-bellied Plovers, Least Sandpipers, Semipalmated Plovers, Dunlins, Greater and Lesser
Yellowlegs, and Short-billed Dowitchers are the most common migrants seen here; other species less common but quite
regular are Western Sandpipers (fall only), Stilt Sandpipers,
Red Knots, Lesser Golden-Plovers (fall only), Sanderlings,
Dunlins (winter also), and Spotted Sandpipers. You should
also look for Upland Sandpipers in the grassy areas near the
buildings, Hudsonian Godwits working the marshy edges,
Baird's and White-rumped Sandpipers mixed in with the Least
and Semipalmated Sandpipers, small but noisy groups of
Long-billed Dowitchers on the flats with the Pectoral Sandpipers, and Whimbrels feeding in the marsh grass. If you are
lucky, you may even turn up a rare species such as a Curlew
Sandpiper.

The marshy areas by the Quicksand Pond breachway are
an excellent place to see Sharp-tailed and Seaside Sparrows
(generally after the first week of May) which, because of their
appearance throughout the summer, presumably breed here,
and "Ipswich" Savannah Sparrows, a chunky, pale race which
is a common winter visitor to Rhode Island from Nova Scotia.
This marsh also offers fine cover for migrating bitterns and
rails; even the rare and elusive Black Rail has been reported
from here.

In addition, Quicksand Pond is a good place to see migrat-
ing waders such as Snowy Egrets, Great Egrets, and Great Blue
Herons. Even an American White Pelican has been seen here.
Terns are worth looking for at Quicksand, too. Common and
Least Terns are the ones most frequently seen, but Roseate and
Black Terns make occasional appearances, as well as Forster's
Terns and Black Skimmers in the fall.

One final note: Quicksand Pond is home to the most
successful Piping Plover breeding colony in the state. This
species is on the endangered species list, so please avoid the
designated nesting areas and watch out for wandering chicks!

4

Sakonnet Point

▼

Specialties: Wintering Seabirds

S.**, Su.*, F.**, W.***

▼

Sakonnet Point, like Quicksand Pond, is located at the southern tip of Little Compton, which places it in a favorable position to attract migrants traveling just off the coast. There are large ponds in this area especially good for finding waterfowl, and Sakonnet Point itself, because it is situated along the coast, is an excellent place to view migrating raptors. There are also several large, rocky islands just south of Sakonnet Point as well as many smaller ones that provide wintering sea ducks with the shelter they need to survive a cold Rhode Island winter. Any birder will find it challenging to see different species swimming among the rocks in a seemingly conscious attempt to hide their identity.

While Sakonnet Point probably offers its best birding in winter, the spring and fall migrations can also be productive. In fact, the whole seaward tip of Little Compton has produced interesting migrants such as Blue Grosbeak, Western Meadowlark, and Peregrine Falcon.

DIRECTIONS:

From the north, follow I-195 east from Providence to Massachusetts Exit 8A, "Tiverton, RI; Newport, RI" (approximately 20 miles). Proceed south on this road (RI 24) to the second Tiverton exit ("Fish Road, Tiverton") and turn left at the end of the exit. Follow this road south for 1.4 miles until you reach the RI 177 intersection—turn right here and pro-

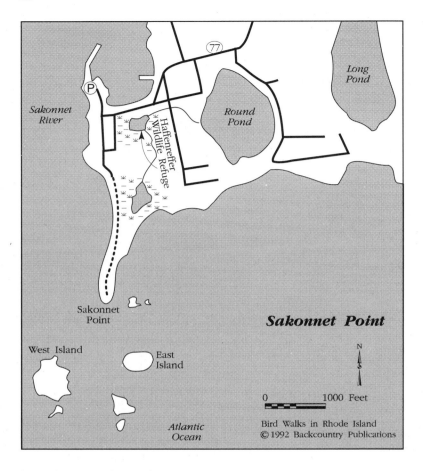

Sakonnet Point

Bird Walks in Rhode Island
© 1992 Backcountry Publications

ceed for 2 miles to RI 77. Turn left (south) onto RI 77 and
follow this road for 10.6 miles until you reach a fork in the
road. Turn right here and continue for another 1.4 miles to the
parking area at Sakonnet Harbor.

From the west, take RI 138 over the Newport Bridge (toll
$2). Continue on RI 138 north for 10.7 miles until you reach
RI 24 north. Follow RI 24 north to the first Tiverton exit
("Tiverton, Little Compton; RI 77 to RI 177"). After reaching
RI 77 south, follow the previous directions under I-195 east.

BIRDING:

Winter birding is the main attraction of Sakonnet Point, and you can begin your day by using your spotting scope at the Sakonnet River and Sakonnet Harbor to look for interesting gulls. Bonaparte's Gulls are common in January—even Glaucous and Iceland Gulls are found here occasionally (usually juvenile birds), and Laughing Gulls make regular appearances throughout the fall migration. Other species that you may see here include Common Loons, Horned Grebes, Red-breasted Mergansers (sometimes large rafts), and Buffleheads, and if you check the rocks that surround the piers, you may see a group of Purple Sandpipers foraging on the mussel-covered substrate.

After you have finished scanning the harbor, you should walk down the dead-end road opposite the entrance to the parking area and follow the trail to the point. Wintering

Roseate Tern

songbirds such as Yellow-rumped Warblers, Song Sparrows, and occasional Gray Catbirds can be found in the thickets along the trail, so be sure to keep your eyes and ears alert as you walk. Interestingly, in the late fall when most inland areas have become cold and inhospitable, late migrant songbirds can often be found near the coast; this is because the ocean's high capacity to hold the summer heat makes the coastal areas the warmest places for birds in late fall. Stragglers to look for include Brown Thrashers, Rufous-sided Towhees and occasionally Dickcissels.

Once you reach the trail that leads to the point (300 feet), be sure to check the small harbor on your right for sea ducks. Oldsquaw, Horned Grebe, Common Goldeneye, and Great Cormorant can all be seen here. Continue walking along this trail until you reach the point. The rocks that surround the point, including East and West Islands as well as Sakonnet Light, are the best places to search for the occasional Common and King Eiders that can be found with the rafts of Surf and White-winged Scoters. These rocks are also a favorite sunning area of the harbor seals which move into the Rhode Island coastal waters in winter.

The open ocean south of Sakonnet Point is also worth a look. Check for Northern Gannets during migration, and in winter check the offshore gulls for the buoyant, bouncing flight of the Black-legged Kittiwakes. Alcids have also been seen from this point; species to look for are Dovekies and Razorbills.

Another winter specialty you may see at Sakonnet Point is the Gyrfalcon. This rare, large, formidable falcon has been seen in the state several times and at Sakonnet Point more than once, particularly in the vicinity of West Island. The best time to look is in December, January, and February. September, October, and November, however, are the best months to look for other migrating falcons such as the American Kestrel, Merlin, and Peregrine Falcon, as well as migrating hawks of which the Sharp-shinned Hawk, Osprey, and Northern Harrier are the most common.

You have completed your tour of Sakonnet Point, but before you leave there are two ponds that you should investigate. The first pond is the Haffenreffer Wildlife Refuge. Haffenreffer is most notable for the Gadwall that breed here, but it is also a good spot to look for migrating American and Least Bitterns, and Rough-legged Hawks (winter only). To reach Haffenreffer continue from the parking area about .1 mile to the refuge on your right.

Approximately 1.4 miles farther east on RI 77 you will see a large pond. This pond is called Round Pond and it is best birded by following the road that skirts it. Many species of waterfowl can be found on this pond during migration— Canada Goose, Snow Goose, Hooded Merganser, American Coot, Ring-necked Duck, Lesser Scaup, and in mid-April, Ruddy Duck (this is one of the few spots in the state where you can find large concentrations of breeding plumage Ruddies).

5

James V. Turner Reservoir

▼

Specialties: Waterfowl

S.***, Su.*, F.***, W.**

▼

Just outside of Rhode Island's capital city is one of the best spots in the state to view migrating waterfowl. The James V. Turner Reservoir, located on the east side of Providence and more commonly known as the East Providence Reservoir, is a certain exception to the idea that good birding areas are rarely located in cities. Consisting of three large ponds, each of which often harbors an interesting array of migrating waterfowl species, this reservoir should definitely be visited by any birder looking for waterfowl in the state of Rhode Island. You might even see a rarity such as the pair of Tundra Swans that spent part of the winter of 1988 here.

DIRECTIONS:

From the north, follow I-95 south to Providence and take the I-195 east exit. Continue on I-195 to Exit 4, "Tauton Avenue, Riverside." Bear left on this exit to Tauton Avenue and US 44 east. Proceed on US 44 east for approximately 2.5 miles until you reach the RI 114 intersection. Turn left at this intersection onto RI 114 north. Continue straight until RI 114 joins RI 1A north (1.5 miles). Turn left at this intersection and follow RI 114 north for .5 mile until you reach Newman Avenue. Turn right and proceed for .5 mile to the causeway dividing the South and Central Ponds.

From the south, follow I-95 north to the I-195 east exit in Providence; from this point, proceed as above.

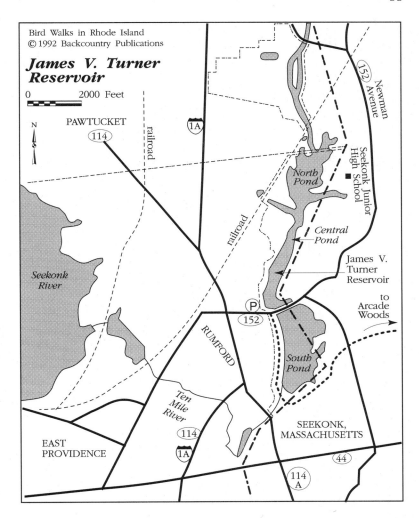

Bird Walks in Rhode Island
© 1992 Backcountry Publications

James V. Turner Reservoir

0   2000 Feet

N

PAWTUCKET
114
railroad
1A
152
Newman Avenue
Seekonk Junior High School
North Pond
Central Pond
James V. Turner Reservoir
railroad
Seekonk River
P
152
RUMFORD
South Pond
to Arcade Woods
Ten Mile River
114
SEEKONK, MASSACHUSETTS
EAST PROVIDENCE
1A
44
114 A

BIRDING:

The causeway overlooking the South and Central Ponds is a good place to start watching for the migrant waterfowl for which this reservoir is most notable. The fall months (September, October, and November) are usually the most productive; March, April, and May are the springtime equivalents.

The best way to bird this area is to start with a quick look at Central Pond—scan this pond for American Wigeon, Ruddy Duck, Ring-necked Duck, and Gadwall. Moreover, Green-winged and Blue-winged Teals can sometimes be found mixed in among them.

After checking the Central Pond, you should turn your attention to South Pond. Usually the South Pond not only has higher concentrations of ducks, but also harbors more species; American Coot, Canvasback, Lesser and Greater Scaups, Ruddy Duck, and Pied-billed Grebe can be common here, particularly during the fall migration.

The best way to bird South Pond is to walk along the trail that begins just at the west side of the causeway. This trail circles the entire South Pond and will, after about three miles, bring you into the Arcade Woods. As you walk along the trail, you will notice small entrances to the pond; you should stop at each of these to look for waterfowl because it seems that each time you look at the pond from a different angle you can see a new species. Many species can be found on this pond on any given day during migration, so search thoroughly because you do not want to miss anything. Uncommon species that you should look for include Common Moorhen, Redhead, and Snow Goose; although these species can sometimes be difficult to find in the state, they are regular transients, and this reservoir is a fine place to look.

If you are looking for a particular species, however, you should be aware that certain species may be common only at specific times of the year. For example, Lesser Scaup and Hooded Merganser seem to be more common at the reservoir in the spring, while Common Merganser, Northern Pintail, and Ruddy Duck are most often seen during the fall.

As you walk along the trail that surrounds South Pond, you may be fortunate enough to startle a Ruffed Grouse—or, more accurately, have one startle you. You may attract the attention of a flock of foraging Black-capped Chickadees, with which you can usually find Downy and Hairy Woodpeckers and White-breasted and Red-breasted Nuthatches, although the latter are usually conspicuous only in the late fall and winter.

If you have decided to make the three-mile walk to the Arcade Woods, you will see that this area is good for migrant land birds as well as summer breeders. The Eastern Kingbird, Red-eyed and Warbling Vireos, Tree Swallow, Belted Kingfisher, and Eastern Screech-Owl have all been found breeding here; in addition, Northern Oriole, Ovenbird, and Wood Thrush also grace the woodland air with their distinctive songs. In the spring and early summer, Fish Crows often pass through these woods, and in the fall large flocks of Blackbirds and American Robins may gather here to roost.

After you return to your car, the next stop is the cattail marshes at the north end of North Pond. To reach this area, continue on Newman Avenue into Seekonk, Massachusetts, for approximately 1.6 miles until you reach the Seekonk Junior High School (on the left). Turn left onto Water Lane and park behind the school. From here you can walk to the water using one of the trails found in this small woodland. Interestingly, American Bittern, Sora, and Virginia Rail were formerly found breeding in these marshes, and may still be found here although there have been no nesting records for the past few years. Other former breeders include Red-shouldered Hawk, Cooper's Hawk, Northern Bobwhite, and Osprey; these species may also be found here occasionally.

Many species of waterfowl can be found on North Pond,

Belted Kingfisher

and some actually seem to prefer it. The Northern Shoveler, for instance, seems to favor these marshy areas and is more commonly found here than on the other ponds.

Another area fairly close to the reservoir that is well worth a look (particularly in the winter) is Watchemocket Cove. This cove can be reached by heading south on Veterans' Memorial Parkway (by bearing right at Exit 4 rather than left) for approximately 1.6 miles until you reach the small bridge which divides the cove into two unequal parts (Watchemocket Cove "north" and Watchemocket Cove "south").

Watchemocket Cove is one of the best places to see Common Black-headed Gulls, with as many as five or six winter adults seen here at low tide on any given winter day. Although the immature Common Black-headed Gulls closely resemble the abundant immature Bonaparte's Gulls, their larger size and pale bills are distinctive as they stand on the ice. This cove is also a good spot to see wintering waterfowl. Several hundred American Wigeons are present here through most of the winter, and you should check these flocks for the regular red-headed Eurasian Wigeon (an adult male has wintered here for the past few years). When all of the inland lakes are frozen, this cove is your best bet for finding wintering Canvasbacks, Hooded Mergansers, and Common Mergansers.

6

Napatree Point

▼

Specialties: Migrant Shorebirds and Hawks

S.***, Su.*, F.***, W.**

▼

Just over a mile long, the Napatree Point sand spit is one of the most productive coastal birding areas in the state. It is the southern boundary of the Little Narragansett Bay, a perfect location to receive many migrant birds in the spring and fall. For example, this point is one of the better places to see Pomarine and Parasitic Jaegers, both of which are very rare in the state. If you are interested in doing some fine coastal birding, getting a good bit of exercise, and walking along a beautiful sand spit, then Napatree Point is the place for you.

DIRECTIONS:

From the north, follow I-95 south from Providence to RI 4 south, Exit 9, "North Kingstown" (13.5 miles). RI 4 south becomes US 1 south after about 6.5 miles. Follow US 1 south for approximately 27 miles until you reach RI 1A south. Continue on RI 1A south for 4.7 miles to a rotary. Turn left at the rotary and proceed 1.8 miles to a stop sign. Turn left at this stop sign and follow this road for .1 mile to Plimpton Hill Road—turn left onto this road for .7 mile until you can go no farther. Turn left and park at the fishing piers on your immediate right. From the parking area to the tip of Napatree Point is a walk of approximately 1.5 miles.

From the west, Exit 1 off I-95 will put you on RI 3 south. Follow RI 3 south until it intersects RI 216 (1.7 miles), and

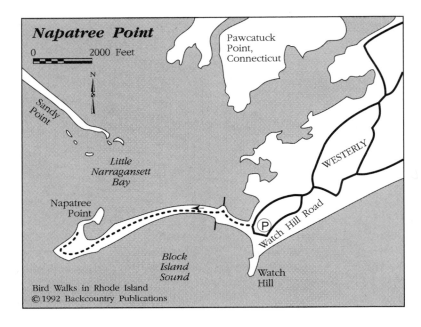

continue on RI 216 south for approximately 6.4 miles to US 1, which runs the length of what Rhode Islanders call the South Shore. After turning right onto US 1 (south), proceed 2 miles to the RI 1A junction. From the RI 1A junction, proceed as above.

BIRDING:

During the spring and fall migrations, many shorebirds can be found working the small tidal pools at the western end of the point. Some of the shorebirds to be found here are Black-bellied Plovers, Lesser Golden-Plovers (fall only), Ruddy Turnstones (often seen on the rocky beach), and Short-billed Dowitchers. Least, Semipalmated, Western, White-rumped, and (rarely) Baird's Sandpipers (fall only) can be found working the sandy areas, particularly in late May and September. Rarities can sometimes also be found at the point—Long-billed Dowitchers, Hudsonian and Marbled Godwits, and if you are really lucky you may even see a Wilson's Phalarope (no recent records) swimming in one of the tidal pools.

In the late summer and early fall many terns begin to wander far from their usual breeding areas, and unusual species can often turn up at coastal spots such as Napatree Point; consequently, Royal Terns, Caspian Terns, Black Terns, Forster's Terns, and Roseate Terns can sometimes be found here, particularly in the fall. It is amusing to watch the Common and Least Terns feeding their fledglings.

The fall migration can be a great time to look for migrating raptors as well. Most of the adult eastern raptors prefer to use the inland migration routes, but the young birds have not yet learned this tactic and use the East Coast as their guide to reach the wintering grounds. Therefore, coastal protuberances such as Napatree Point offer a fine vantage point from which to watch the impressive southward migrations of these hawks. The best weather conditions for fall hawk migration are cold fronts followed by northwest winds.

The start of the 1.5-mile hike to Napatree Point

Some of the hawk species which can be seen in large numbers following these weather conditions are Sharp-shinned Hawk, American Kestrel, Broad-winged Hawk, Osprey, Northern Harrier, Red-shouldered Hawk, and, of less frequent but regular occurrence, Cooper's Hawk, Peregrine Falcon, Merlin, and even an occasional Northern Goshawk. In the fall, buzzing flocks of swallows can also be found here—species include Tree, Barn, Bank, and Rough-winged Swallows; even Cliff Swallows and Purple Martins can be seen gathering for their flight south.

In the winter, after the Sharp-tailed Sparrow's buzzy song can no longer be heard and the Fish Crows that frequent the area have dispersed, Napatree Point is still worth a visit for wintering birds. All of the sea birds that can normally be found in Rhode Island waters have been found here. Common Loons, Horned Grebes, Common Goldeneyes, and Red-breasted Mergansers are the most regular winter residents, but Red-necked Grebes, Red-throated Loons, and Common Eiders make occasional appearances. The rare species seen from this point include Pomarine Jaeger, Harlequin Duck, King Eider, and Barrow's Goldeneye. Even loons of the Pacific Loon–Arctic Loon complex have been reported. Other wintering birds to look for are Purple Sandpipers and Brant, both of which are often found around the rocks of the point; Horned Larks and Snow Buntings can often be seen feeding along the beach. Wintering shorebirds (such as Dunlins and Sanderlings) are also common here, so be cautious as you walk; patience may reward you with close observations.

If you decide to visit Napatree Point during the summer, be sure not to disturb its breeding birds which include Piping Plovers, Common and Least Terns, Ospreys, and American Oystercatchers.

7

Block Island

▼

Specialties: Fall Migrants

S.**, Su.**, F.***, W.**

▼

Because of Block Island's size, extensive roadways, sparse tree
cover, and geographic location, it is one of the best birding
spots in the state. It is also probably the one place that brings
in more out-of-state birders than any other location. Aware of
its ability to produce rare and uncommon species every fall,
many birders make the annual pilgrimage out to the island in
September and October to look for seldom-seen species such
as Gray-cheeked Thrushes and Philadelphia Vireos.

The ferry ride to Block Island from Galilee is a very
pleasant one and only lasts about one hour. Oftentimes you
can find interesting birds on this trip too.

DIRECTIONS:

To reach Block Island you must take the Block Island Ferry,
which leaves from the Galilee boat docks in Narragansett,
Rhode Island. At the time of this writing, the cost for one
passenger is $10 same-day round trip, and the cost for one
vehicle one way is $20.25. You must make reservations well
in advance to transport a vehicle. For information or reserva-
tions call (401) 783-4613.

BIRDING:

Block Island is a fairly small island, approximately three miles
wide by seven miles long, with roughly twenty-eight miles of

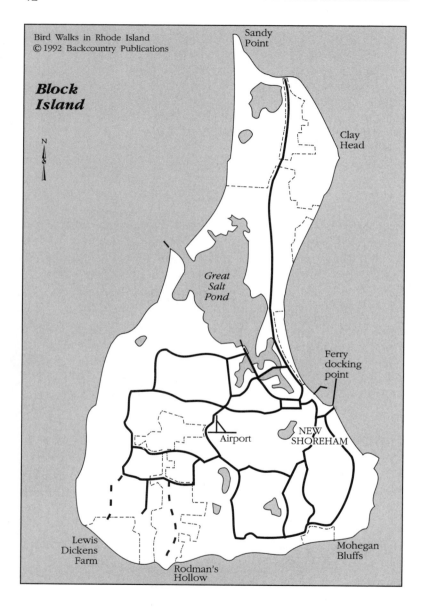

Bird Walks in Rhode Island
© 1992 Backcountry Publications

**Block
Island**

N

Sandy
Point

Clay
Head

*Great
Salt
Pond*

Ferry
docking
point

Airport

NEW
SHOREHAM

Lewis
Dickens
Farm

Rodman's
Hollow

Mohegan
Bluffs

paved roads. To supplement this chapter's map of the island and its major roads, you can purchase a more detailed map at one of the local convenience stores near the ferry dock.

As noted, Block Island is one of the finest fall migrant traps on the East Coast—the best months are late August through early November. When a cold front moves through followed by northwest winds, most of the migrants that were bumped offshore during the night pitch down on the island to refuel for the next night's migration. During these conditions (this is a recurring fall weather pattern), you may find some interesting species such as Northern Wheatear and Hudsonian Godwit. Occasionally the opposite weather pattern will have just as profound an effect. For example, a warm front moving up from the south sometimes pushes more southerly occurring birds into our area, such as Yellow-throated Warbler, Kentucky Warbler, Black-necked Stilt, and even the rare Fork-tailed Flycatcher from South America.

The Audubon Society of Rhode Island sponsors a weekend trip to the island in late September or early October; these trips are led by some of the most knowledgeable birders in the area, and if you have the opportunity to go along, you will undoubtedly see some fascinating species. If, however, you cannot be a part of this trip, you should make a point to visit the island on your own sometime during the fall migration.

Careful and thorough birding should produce many of the migrant warblers common in eastern North America—species such as Nashville, Tennessee, Bay-breasted, Wilson's, Magnolia, and Northern Parula Warblers, to name just a few. In addition, sparrows such as Lincoln's, Lark, White-crowned, Vesper, and Dickcissel can be found on the island in the fall. Vireos, which you should look for, include Solitary, Yellow-throated, and Philadelphia. Incidently, the Philadelphia Vireo is rarely detected during the spring migration, so the best time to find this bird is in the fall, and Block Island is a good place to look.

As you drive, bicycle, or walk around the island, be sure to check the telephone wires and fence posts for migrant

flycatchers, including out-of-range species such as Western
Kingbird and Ash-throated Flycatcher. Even the rare Fork-
tailed Flycatcher has been seen here. Also, thoroughly check
all blackbird flocks for the regular fall appearance of the
Yellow-headed Blackbird among the Rusty and Red-winged
Blackbirds, Common Grackles, Brown-headed Cowbirds,
and Bobolinks with which it is usually found.

Some of the other species seen on the island during the fall
migration include these warblers: Cape May, Black-throated
Blue, Black-throated Green, Cerulean, Pine, Prairie, Palm,
Chestnut-sided, Blackpoll, Black-and-white, American Redstart, Common Yellowthroat, Hooded Warbler, Yellow-
breasted Chat, Worm-eating and Blackburnian Warblers, and
Canada and Mourning Warblers. Both Northern and Louisiana Waterthrushes and the very rare Connecticut Warbler
have been found in the low brush present on much of the
island, as well as Rose-breasted and Blue Grosbeaks. Hermit,
Swainson's, and Gray-cheeked Thrushes (rarely; the first
week in October) all stop on the island on their way south.

The fall is also the best time to see migrant raptors such as
Peregrine Falcons (common some years), Merlins, Cooper's
and Sharp-shinned Hawks, and an occasional Northern Goshawk. Be sure to check the marshy areas on the island for
migrating bitterns, rails, and waders.

Winter birding on Block Island can also be productive. A
trip to the island between the months of November and
February may produce such species as Black-legged Kittiwake,
Northern Gannet, and alcids such as Razorbill and Dovekie—
and these are just on the ferry ride over. After reaching the
island, you should search all gull flocks for Glaucous and
Iceland Gulls as well as occasional Lesser Black-backed Gulls.
You should also check for owls on the island. Sandy Point has
been very productive in the past for Snowy Owls, with as many
as four birds having been seen at one time. Barn Owls can also
be found here. During the summer a very few pairs breed under
the cliffs, spending the winter in the large pine roosts of the
southwest part of the island. Long-eared Owls and Northern
Saw-whet Owls have been found here, so look carefully as you

*Fork-Tailed
Flycatcher*

walk through the pines; they can often be very difficult to spot
among the branches.

The Block Island coast should also be checked for wintering ducks. Common Goldeneyes and Red-breasted Mergan-

sers are the most common ducks seen off the coast. However, if the sea is particularly rough, you may find some of the wintering sea ducks hiding in the large unfrozen ponds on the island along with wintering American Black Ducks, Mallards, Green-winged Teals, and occasional Northern Pintails.

Summertime on Block Island is a time when most birders stay away because of the hordes of people who come to the island, but birding here in the spring and summer can be rewarding, for there are several interesting breeding birds, particularly the Grasshopper Sparrow and Upland Sandpiper. Although very few Grasshopper Sparrows have been located in recent years, they probably still breed in small numbers on the southwestern part of the island, primarily on private property which makes access to them restricted. But if you are on the southwestern part and you listen for its buzzy song, you may be rewarded with a glimpse of this rare sparrow.

The Upland Sandpiper is, unfortunately, another story. A nest of this species has not been found on the island for several years, although some people believe that it still nests here. Some other nesting species of particular note are Black-crowned Night-Heron, Northern Harrier, American Oyster-catcher, Bank Swallow, and Savannah Sparrow.

Quonochontaug

▼

Specialties: Shorebirds

S.***, Su.*, F.***, W.**

▼

Located off US 1 just west of Ninigret Pond and just east of Napatree Point, Quonochontaug is another good birding area sandwiched between two other good birding areas, and it is easy to stop at all three places in a short amount of time.

Quonochontaug is best known as a prime shorebird and wader location, because the extensive salt marshes provide ample feeding grounds for large numbers of species. One particularly nice benefit to birding at Quonochontaug is that even during the summer the beach-going crowds are moderate and you can still do some fairly good birding at this large pond.

DIRECTIONS:

From the north, follow I-95 south from Providence for 13.5 miles to RI 4 south, Exit 9, "North Kingstown." RI 4 south becomes US 1 south after about 6.5 miles. Follow US 1 south for approximately 25.1 miles to Quonochontaug Road: "Quonochontaug, West Beach Area." Continue on Quono-chontaug Road (south) for 1.4 miles until you reach a fork in the road; bear right at this fork and continue until you reach the Quonochontaug parking area.

From the west, Exit 1 off I-95 will put you on RI 3 south. Follow RI 3 south until it intersects RI 216 (1.7 miles), and

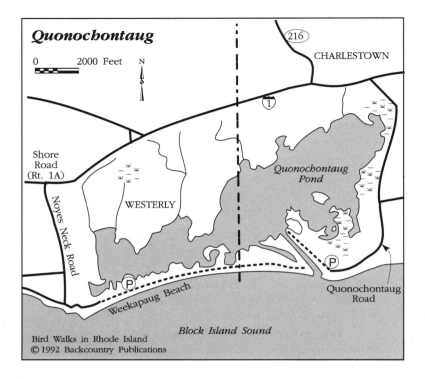

continue on RI 216 south for approximately 6.4 miles to US
1. After turning left onto US 1 (north), follow this road for .4
mile to the "Quonochontaug, West Beach Area" exit and
proceed as above.

    Another access area can be reached by continuing on US
1 south 1.9 miles past the Quonochontaug Road exit to RI 1A
south. Take your second left after turning onto RI 1A south
(1 mile) to Noyes Neck Road. Follow this road for approximately 1 mile, through a stop sign (remembering to stop at the
stop sign), then bear left, and continue for another .3 mile to
the Quonochontaug Conservation Commission parking area.
From here you must walk along the dirt road to gain access to
the pond and its abundant bird life.

BIRDING:

Quonochontaug is most notable for the large concentrations of shorebirds that gather here during the spring and fall migrations. Many species have been seen foraging on the mud flats in the marshy area—common species include Black-bellied Plover, Short-billed Dowitcher, and Semipalmated Sandpiper. Furthermore, Greater and Lesser Yellowlegs can be abundant here. Other particularly notable species are Ruff, Curlew Sandpiper, Hudsonian and Marbled Godwits, Wilson's Pharalope, and Buff-breasted Sandpiper; the possibility of finding any one of these species makes a trip to Quono-chontaug well worth the effort.

Both American and Least Bitterns, as well as Clapper Rail, have been seen here during migration, and it is not uncommon for individuals to linger into the early winter, though it usually takes some rustling through the marsh to scare them up. When

Looking East over the Quonochontaug salt marsh

the tide is low and the mud flats are exposed, Snowy Egrets, Great Egrets, Great Blue Herons, and other species (such as Little Blue Herons) often gather here to feed on the small fish trapped in the tidal pools. Even Tricolored Herons have been found here. If you are lucky and are awake early enough, you may catch a glimpse of a Black-crowned Night-Heron flying off to his day roost, or you may even see the Yellow-crowned Night-Heron that sometimes passes through.

In the fall Quonochontaug also attracts terns to its sandy beaches. Common Terns are the most abundant along with Least Terns, but Royal and Black Terns are often seen, as well as an occasional Black Skimmer. Migrant hawks also pass through this area in fairly large numbers; a species of particular note that has been seen with considerable regularity is the Peregrine Falcon. Other species that can be seen include migrant swallows (even the Purple Martin), and an occasional small, very fast Ruby-throated Hummingbird (early September is a good time to look for them).

Although summertime is usually rather slow for birding at Quonochontaug, because the people who come to Rhode Island beaches keep many of the marsh birds away, this marsh is not totally devoid of bird life. Quonochontaug is home to breeding populations of Sharp-tailed and Seaside Sparrows whose buzzy calls make the marsh seem teeming with large insects. These sparrows are not the only summer residents; Red-winged Blackbirds and Common Grackles are common here. In fact, during the summer of 1986 a group of five Boat-tailed Grackles was found here. Why they were here no one is certain, but they stayed about two months and made viewing easy for those who went to find them.

9

Trustom Pond
National Wildlife Refuge

▼

Specialties: Waterfowl, Land Birds, Shorebirds

S.*, Su.*, F.**, W.**

▼

Trustom Pond has always been one of my favorite birding areas in Rhode Island because it provides a great diversity of habitats through which to look for birds. From shorebirds and waterfowl to land birds and marsh birds, Trustom can produce them all. It is one of several National Wildlife Refuges in the state, and the care and protection given to land of this status is evident. If you like to take walks through fields and forests and look over large ponds for waterfowl, then Trustom Pond is the place to visit.

DIRECTIONS:

From the north, follow I-95 south from Providence for 13.5 miles to RI 4 south, Exit 9, "North Kingstown." RI 4 south becomes US 1 south after about 6.5 miles. Continue on US 1 south for approximately 17.2 miles to the "Moonstone Beach" exit. Follow Moonstone Beach Road south for 1.1 miles until you come to a four-way stop. Turn right here onto Matunuck Schoolhouse Road, and proceed .7 mile to the Trustom Pond National Wildlife Refuge on your left. Park in the parking area and follow the trails to the pond.

From the west, Exit 1 off I-95 will put you on RI 3 south.

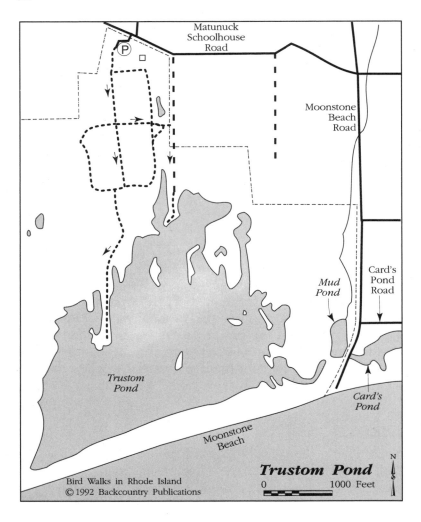

Follow RI 3 south until it intersects RI 216 (1.7 miles), and continue on RI 216 south for approximately 6.4 miles to US 1. After turning left onto US 1 (north), follow this road for 8.6 miles to the "Moonstone Beach" exit and proceed as above.

BIRDING:

Trustom Pond is a fine place to see wintering waterfowl, migrant land birds, hawks, and shorebirds. Greater Scaup and large concentrations of American Black Ducks can be found here in the winter; these wintering flocks should be checked for other wintering species such as Northern Pintail, Green-winged Teal, Lesser Scaup and Northern Shoveler. In addition, mid-April is the best time to see small groups of Redhead and Blue-winged Teal, both of which can be difficult to find in this state.

The trails leading to the pond can be productive for migrant land birds. Late fall migrants that you are likely to see include Eastern Bluebird, Hermit Thrush, Brown Thrasher, and Rufous-sided Towhee. In the winter, however, the only sounds you will probably hear in these woods are the cawing of American Crows and the call notes of Tufted Titmice, Black-capped Chickadees, White-throated Sparrows, and Golden-crowned Kinglets. But once you reach the water's edge, you can usually find large groups of waterfowl through which to search for oddities.

Also, Trustom Pond is one of the better places in the state to see wandering Bald and possibly Golden Eagles—one or two eagles are reported from this area every spring and fall, so a trip to look for these wanderers is well worth the effort. Other birds of prey are likely to be seen passing over this refuge in the fall; these include Sharp-shinned and Cooper's Hawks, and Red-shouldered and Broad-winged Hawks (sometimes uncommon in migration).

The large field you will see shortly after you begin walking along the trail often harbors large flocks of blackbirds in the fall, and you should look for Bobolinks and Eastern Meadowlarks mixed in with them (an occasional Yellow-headed Blackbird can sometimes be found in a large flock such as this one). Eastern Kingbirds and Great Crested Flycatchers are common spring visitors to the wooded areas of Trustom, both often staying on to breed. In early spring you can even listen to American Woodcocks as they whistle and whinny while doing their courtship flight. The walk from the parking area to the pond not only takes you through some excellent birding habitat but also will bring you to a fine waterfowl and occasional shorebird gathering spot.

Two other areas near the Trustom Pond National Wildlife Refuge that you might want to see are the fields around Card's Pond Road and Card's Pond itself. Many geese and waterfowl can be found on Card's Pond in the spring and fall; if the water levels are low, this area can be host to some large shorebird flocks. Even a Curlew Sandpiper has been found here.

The corn fields around Card's Pond Road can sometimes harbor large flocks of geese. For instance, in the fall of 1988 a flock of seventeen Snow Geese, two hundred Canada Geese, and one Greater White-fronted Goose was found here, and again in 1990 a Greater White-fronted Goose was found here with a group of Canada and Snow Geese. The telephone wires

Looking south over Card's Pond

Piping Plover

along this road are worth a look in the fall for American Kestrels and vagrant Western Kingbirds. In the winter you should look for the rare Northern Shrikes that sometimes wander far south of their normal wintering range, and Rough-legged Hawks that can occasionally be seen hunting over the grassy fields and marshes.

10

Ninigret National Wildlife Refuge

▼

Specialties: Shorebirds, Waders, Migrants

S.***, Su.***, F.***, W.**

▼

This wildlife refuge, like Trustom Pond, has a vast array of habitats through which to look for birds. Most of the refuge is an old airport, and the unkempt runways are still evident at the beginnings and endings of many of the trails. A large airport so close to this pond probably at one time discouraged most species of wildlife from inhabiting the area. But in the many years since the airport's closing, the vegetation has run rampant and the native wildlife has certainly returned in full force. Good birds are to be found at this refuge at all seasons, and good butterflies are to be found in the spring and summer.

DIRECTIONS:

From the north, follow I-95 south from Providence to RI 4 south, Exit 9, "North Kingstown." RI 4 south becomes US 1 south after about 6.5 miles. Follow US 1 south for approximately 23.1 miles to the "Ninigret Wildlife Refuge" exit (not the "Ninigret Park" exit; you will stop there later). After taking this exit follow the signs to the parking area (200 feet). At the right side of the parking area there is a kiosk on which you can see the entire refuge mapped out with trails. Note: there is a fee charged here in the summer, usually from Memorial Day weekend in late May to Labor Day weekend in early September.

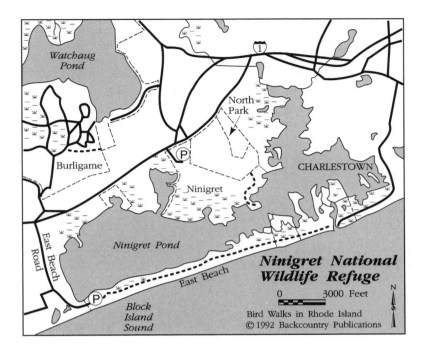

From the west, Exit 1 off I-95 will put you on RI 3 south. Follow RI 3 south until it intersects RI 216 (1.7 miles), and continue on RI 216 south for approximately 6.4 miles to US 1. After turning left onto US 1 (north), follow this road for 2.6 miles to the exit at "Ninigret Wildlife Refuge" and proceed as above.

BIRDING:

From this parking area there are several trails which you can walk along, all starting from the same point. Second-growth woodlands, small fields, and marshy areas are habitats that you will find at Ninigret, and, if lucky, you will find the Rhode Island breeding birds appropriate for them. Ninigret's breeding birds include Yellow-breasted Chat, American Woodcock, White-eyed Vireo, Blue-winged Warbler, Sharp-tailed Sparrow, Brown Thrasher, Common Yellowthroat, American Goldfinch, Cedar Waxwing, and Marsh Wren. In the spring, however, these areas not only are alive with the songs of the breeding birds but also echo with the songs and call notes of many migrants; Chestnut-sided, Bay-breasted, and Palm Warblers, Solitary and Yellow-throated Vireos stop occasionally, and even a few species of flycatcher including Least, Alder, and Willow Flycatchers are among the waves of migrants that sometimes pass through.

As you walk along the trails, be sure to check for Green-backed Herons, Marsh Wrens, Common Snipes, Pied-billed Grebes, and American Coots skulking along the edges of the *Phragmites* grass. Also check the thickets thoroughly for migrant land birds; coastal areas can often be a haven for these transients.

Brown Thrasher

Although summer and spring birding at Ninigret can be productive, the best birding is in the fall, particularly during the peak shorebird migration from August through September. To reach one of the fine vantage points from which to search Ninigret Pond for shorebirds, follow US 1 south for 1.5 miles past the wildlife refuge exit to "East Beach Road." Continue on East Beach Road for 1.5 miles (bearing left) until you reach the Ninigret Conservation Area parking lot. Park here and walk along a portion of the pond's edge. Outstanding shorebirds that have been seen here are American Avocet, Curlew Sandpiper, Wilson's Phalarope, and Whimbrel, as well as Baird's and White-rumped Sandpipers. Moreover, Ninigret Pond is one of the best places in the state to see Stilt Sandpipers and Marbled Godwits (rare). Other more common species that you are likely to see in the spring and fall are Black-bellied Plover, Lesser Golden-Plover (fall only), Red Knot, Ruddy Turnstone, Short-billed Dowitcher, and the various "Peep" sandpipers: Least, Western, Semipalmated, Baird's, White-rumped.

In addition, Ninigret Pond can be productive for waders, terns, and occasionally migrant hawks in the late summer and fall. Royal and Caspian Terns, Black Skimmers, and Black Terns seem to be regular visitors in the fall, and Forster's and Roseate Terns are not uncommon. In the fall, terns can be especially difficult to distinguish, so be sure to check all of them thoroughly before dismissing any. Waders found here include Great Egret, Snowy Egret, Little Blue Heron, and even Yellow-crowned Night-Heron. And the fall migration usually brings some interesting raptors over the refuge. On a good day, Sharp-shinned and Cooper's Hawks, Northern Harriers, and possibly Peregrine Falcons, Merlins, or Northern Goshawks can be seen flying overhead.

In the winter, Ninigret Pond is often loaded with wintering ducks, particularly Common Goldeneye, Canada Goose, and Red-breasted Merganser. Furthermore, the largest concentrations of Bufflehead in the state usually occur at Ninigret. You should also look for rare gulls such as Glaucous and

Iceland Gulls; the only recorded sighting of Ivory Gull in Rhode Island was made here. The open-ocean part of this refuge is worth a look for sea ducks. In November 1988 a Brown Pelican was photographed from this area along with over 2,000 Northern Gannets.

Ninigret Park can be reached by heading north on US 1 to the "Ninigret Park" exit. The park also provides a good access point from which to view the pond if you follow the park road to its end and walk to the observation tower overlooking the pond.

11

Great Swamp
Management Area

▼

Specialties: Migrant Land Birds

S.**, Su.*, F.**, W.*

▼

The Great Swamp Management Area is a state-owned tract of land intended to boost Rhode Island's native waterfowl population. Species such as Wood Ducks, Tree Swallows, Ospreys and Red-winged Blackbirds are amazingly abundant in the summertime as well as a vast assortment of other nesting species. There are many insects here, and many interesting species of plants and butterflies. The area has always given me the feeling that I was in a more southerly swamp; the heat, humidity, bugs, and *Usnea* lichen hanging off the trees all work together to create this image in my mind. Perhaps you will feel the same way after a visit.

DIRECTIONS:

From the north, follow I-95 south from Providence for 13.5 miles to RI 4 south, Exit 9, "North Kingstown." RI 4 south becomes US 1 south after about 6.5 miles. Follow US 1 south for approximately 6 miles to RI 138 west (turn right at the Tavern on the Hill Restaurant). Continue on RI 138 west for 5.3 miles to the Great Swamp Management Area sign (just past the RI 110 intersection). Turn left at this sign and follow this road for .8 mile until you reach Great Neck Road. Turn left onto Great Neck Road and proceed for 1 mile (on dirt) to the

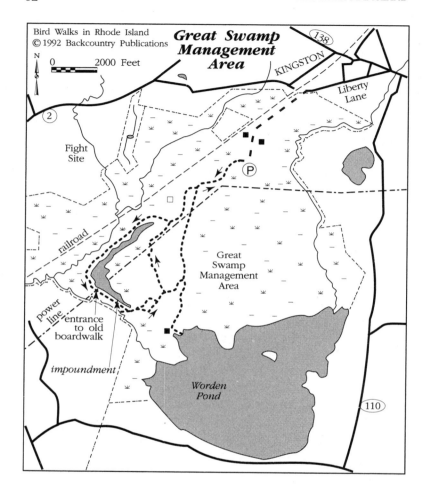

parking area. Another access can be reached by following RI
138 west for 1.3 miles, past the first entrance, to RI 2. Turn
left onto RI 2 south and continue on this road for 1.6 miles to
the Great Swamp Fight Monument sign. Turn left at this sign
and follow this dirt road .8 mile to the Great Fight Monument
and park there. From either of these entrances you can pick up
trails that will lead you through much of the management area.

From the west, Exit 3A off I-95 (approximately 6.5 miles from the Connecticut–Rhode Island border) will put you on RI 138 east. Follow RI 138 east for roughly 9 miles to the Great Swamp Management area sign—just before the RI 110 junction—and proceed as above.

BIRDING:

The Great Swamp is an area with many trails through some highly varied and productive birding habitat. From either of the access areas you will find trails that will lead you through wooded upland areas and lowland swampy and marshy areas. A word of caution: Because of the stagnant water in a large portion of this area, the biting insects are well represented; therefore, birding should be done in the early spring, late fall, or winter. Summer birding is (for most people) out of the question.

In the spring this area is often worth a visit to look for early migrants. Palm, Pine and Prairie Warblers usually turn up fairly early here, as well as Black-and-white Warblers and the five swallows and one martin species that occur regularly in Rhode Island.

The best way to bird this area is to start birding at the parking area off Great Neck Road. If you follow the dirt trail from this parking lot to the power lines and turn right, you will be led through some fine upland birding areas and will eventually come to the boardwalk (if you want to call it that) over the Great Swamp.

The best time to visit the swamp is between April 15 and May 15. In early May from the parking area you should be able to hear Ovenbirds, Great Crested Flycatchers, Black-and-white Warblers, and Brown Thrashers, to name only a few. The walk from the parking area to the power lines can also produce interesting species. For example, Rusty Blackbirds are common in the marshy areas in late April but are dwindling in number by the first week in May; Blue-winged Teal can be flushed from the marsh; and Yellow-bellied Sapsuckers can occasionally be heard as they slowly and methodically tap holes in the trees. Common Yellowthroats, Yellow Warblers, and Swamp Sparrows are common along this stretch of road as well.

After reaching the power lines, turn right and follow the trail to the boardwalk. Along the way you will pass between mature stands of mixed coniferous and deciduous woodlands. Migrant warblers can be seen here as they stop to feed on the abundant insect life. Species to look for include Chestnut-sided, Parula, Black-throated Green, Cape May, Bay-breasted, Nashville, Tennessee, Canada, Mourning (late spring), Kentucky and Prothonotary (rarely), and Wilson's Warbler. All of the northeastern vireos can be found here: Red-eyed, White-eyed, Yellow-throated, Solitary, Warbling, and Philadelphia (fall only).

Thrushes pass through in fair number as well; Hermit, Wood, Gray-cheeked (one record), Swainson's, and Veery have all been found.

View from the trail surrounding the impoundment

Migrants, however, are not the only attraction here. Although some of the above-mentioned species do breed here (Chestnut-sided Warbler and Wood Thrush), many others can be found, particularly in mid-May when most birds have already begun setting up territories. Species to look for (if you can stand the insects) include Eastern Bluebird, Eastern Wood-Pewee, Least Flycatcher, Brown Creeper, Indigo Bunting, House Wren, Carolina Wren, and Blue-gray Gnatcatcher. These woodlands have also produced such interesting species as Pileated Woodpecker, Northern Bobwhite, and Cerulean Warbler.

After you have scanned the upland areas for migrants and summer residents, you may want to attempt to walk along the badly deteriorating boardwalk over the swamp. Be careful: It is passable only about halfway. In early May the Swamp Sparrows are busy claiming territories and defending them; in the morning you'll hear the trilling songs of what seems like millions of them. Red-winged Blackbirds and Common Grackles are usually seen here in the spring and summer, and the flocks of returning Tree Swallows can be very impressive. Mixed in with the Tree Swallows you should look for other returning swallows such as Barn, Bank, Northern Rough-winged, and Cliff. Even Purple Martins pass through this area in early spring. Furthermore, waterfowl are common in the marsh in the early spring—Wood Ducks, which breed here amid the Canada Geese, are the most common ducks in this swamp, but Green-winged and Blue-winged Teals, Ring-necked Ducks, and even Buffleheads can be found here at the right time.

The Ospreys will delight you with their enormous stick nests placed atop the power-line poles, and their piercing cries will warn you that they have young. When the Ospreys begin calling, their loud monotonous sounds are usually enough to stimulate the Virginia Rails to begin their two-noted clicking song.

Even in the winter this swamp can provide some interesting birding. Owls are easiest to hear at this time of year because their calls are not concealed behind the noise of the numerous insects and frogs whose calls fill the summer nights. Moreover, a big wild area like this will often contain large flocks of wintering sparrows such as White-throated Sparrow, Dark-eyed Junco, and Tree Sparrow. Other sounds you are likely to hear in the winter are the thin, triplet whistles of the Golden-crowned Kinglet, and the distinctive nasal honking of the White-breasted Nuthatch, all reminding you that there is still life in the seemingly lifeless winter woodland.

12

Burlingame State Park

▼

Specialties: Breeding Birds

S.**, Su.**, F.**, W.**

▼

If you are a birder interested in finding land birds in Rhode Island, Burlingame State Park is a fine place to start looking. Composed of a typical eastern deciduous forest, the woodlands of Burlingame have all of the species characteristic of this forest type and also provide some beautiful trails for hiking.

DIRECTIONS:

From the north, follow I-95 south from Providence for 13.5 miles to RI 4 south, Exit 9, "North Kingstown." RI 4 south becomes US 1 south after about 6.5 miles. Follow US 1 south for approximately 22.7 miles to the "King's Factory Road" exit. Continue north on King's Factory Road for 3.2 miles to Buckeye Brook Road. Turn left onto this road and drive for .6 mile to a large dirt road on your left. You can follow this road south for 1.5 miles to the north end of Watchaug Pond and a camping area, or you can continue west on Buckeye Brook Road for another .2 mile to another dirt road on your right. This dirt road is the Clawson Trail. Across the street you will find the start of the White Trail; however, if you wish to explore some of the other trails, follow Buckeye Brook Road west for another .5 mile past the White Trail to the Yellow Trail, which later intersects the Blue Trail. Whichever trail you decide to follow, you will quickly find yourself in the middle of an excellent birding area.

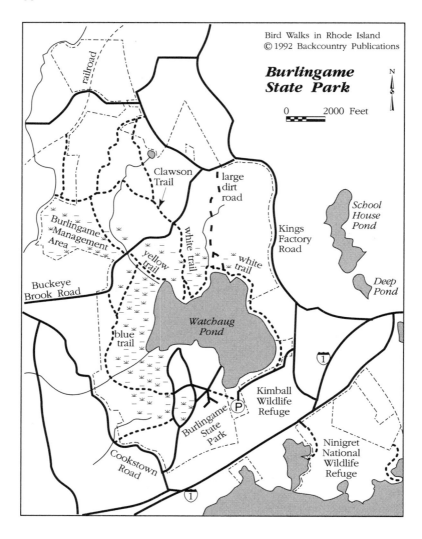

From the west, Exit 1 off I-95 will put you on RI 3 south. Follow RI 3 south until it intersects RI 216 (1.7 miles), and continue on RI 216 south for approximately 5.3 miles to Buckeye Brook Road on your left. Proceed as above, but the trails will now be on the opposite side of the road, and you will see the Yellow Trail first instead of the access road to Watchaug Pond.

BIRDING:

The most productive birding walk at Burlingame I have found is the loop around Watchaug Pond. You can start this loop by finding the White Trail and following it clockwise around the pond to the Blue Trail, and eventually to the Yellow Trail which will bring you back to Buckeye Brook Road.

Burlingame is a park in which to search for breeding birds. Both the Northern and Louisiana Waterthrushes breed here; although the latter prefers fast-running streams, the Northern Waterthrush can be seen most often by the stagnant pools of water typically found in a moist lowland forest such as this. Also Golden-crowned Kinglets have nested here (an uncommon breeder in Rhode Island)—look for them in the conifers, particularly the spruces, which they favor. And the careful observer may even be fortunate enough to stumble across a Whip-poor-will nest concealed in the leaf litter on the ground. If you are content with simply listening for the breeding birds, though, rather than looking for nests, you will be delighted by

Fox Sparrow

the sounds of the many Wood and Hermit Thrushes, White-eyed and Yellow-throated Vireos, Blue-winged and Prairie Warblers, and Field and Chipping Sparrows. One of my favorite woodland sounds, commonly heard here, is the emphatic "wheep" of the Great Crested Flycatcher. This call is so distinctive, yet sounds so labored, that you cannot help admiring the bird for its efforts. As you walk through these woods, you will soon find that if you do not already know your eastern bird songs there can be great joy in learning them.

One of the interesting places you will see is the swampy area. It is located along the Blue Trail just before it intersects the Yellow Trail. There used to be a boardwalk over this area; due to neglect, however, it is considerably dilapidated. The swamp is not extensive, but during the summer months you may still find species such as Swamp Sparrows, Green-backed Herons, and Yellow Warblers.

One important point to remember about Burlingame State Park is that it is mainly an area to look for breeding birds, although, as with any wooded area, migrant land birds can be found here at the appropriate time. Therefore, you need not make many trips to the area. Breeding birds will remain through most of the summer, and because of the length of the loop around Watchaug Pond (about 7.5 miles) and the time involved (depending upon your walking pace, anywhere from 1 to 3 hours), it is best to make only a few trips a year and plan to spend some time. Watchaug Pond is often worth a look in spring and fall for migrating waterfowl.

One area along the loop that you do not necessarily have to hike several miles to reach is the Kimball Wildlife Refuge, to which you can easily drive. To reach this area continue on US 1 south for approximately 1 mile past King's Factory Road to the Burlingame State Park Picnic Area. After exiting, follow this road for .2 mile and turn left onto Montauk Road. Proceed on Montauk Road for .6 mile to Watchaug Pond; turn left at the pond and follow this road .5 mile to the Kimball parking area. Kimball is, like Burlingame State Park, an excellent place to find breeding birds. However, Kimball is a good spot to find wintering birds as well. The thickets that surround the parking area often harbor several wintering species, including White-throated Sparrows, Tree Sparrows, Dark-eyed Juncos, Downy and Hairy Woodpeckers, and occasionally White-crowned Sparrows (rare in winter) and Eastern Bluebirds. Also, the woodlands of Kimball can sometimes provide birders with sightings of winter finches such as Evening Grosbeaks, Pine Siskins, and White-winged Crossbills.

13

Arcadia Management Area

▼

Specialties: Migrant Land Birds

S.***, Su.***, F.***, W.**

▼

One of the largest birding areas in Rhode Island, the Arcadia Management Area is certainly also one of the most diversified and productive upland birding areas. Any birder wishing to find most of this state's birds will have to make a trip to Arcadia, for it is here that several species of birds are most easily found—for example, Acadian and Least Flycatchers. Whether you are looking to add new birds to your Rhode Island state or year list or you are just out to see different species of birds, Arcadia is certainly worth a visit.

DIRECTIONS:

From the north, follow I-95 south from Providence for approximately 23.5 miles to Exit 5, "RI 102 south." Follow RI 102 south to the RI 3 intersection and turn right (south).Continue south on RI 3 for 2.6 miles to RI 165 west. From here directions to the individual trails will be given.

From the west, follow I-95 north for approximately 6 miles past the Connecticut–Rhode Island boundary to exit 3B, "RI 138 west." Continue west on RI 138 for about 1 mile to RI 3 north. Follow RI 3 north for 5.5 miles to RI 165 west.

Arcadia Management Area is a huge tract of state-owned land that is loaded with trails and access points. I will give directions to four different trails; the map with this chapter will help you find your way to these trails but does not show

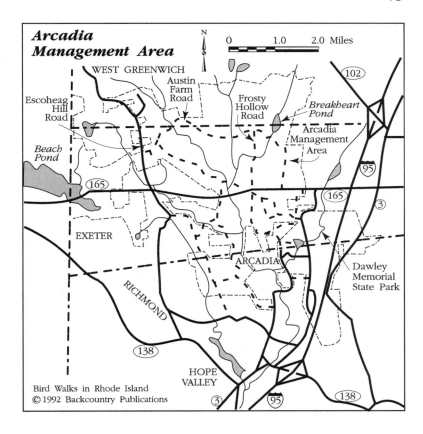

Arcadia Management Area

N

0   1.0   2.0 Miles

WEST GREENWICH

Austin
Farm
Road

Escoheag
Hill
Road

Frosty
Hollow
Road

*Breakheart
Pond*

Arcadia
Management
Area

102

95

*Beach
Pond*

165

165

3

EXETER

ARCADIA

Dawley
Memorial
State Park

RICHMOND

138

HOPE
VALLEY

Bird Walks in Rhode Island
© 1992 Backcountry Publications

3

95

138

the trails themselves. You will soon find, however, that there are many other trails which can be equally productive for birds. A good book that lists eleven different trails through the Arcadia Management Area is Ken Weber's *Walks and Rambles in Rhode Island.* The four trails that I use most frequently are:

The Arcadia Trail—To reach the Arcadia Trail, follow RI 3 south for 2.9 miles past the RI 102 intersection to Dawley Memorial State Park. You should park at the big brown log cabin on your right, for behind this structure you can pick up the Arcadia Trail. The trail that you will follow is yellow-blazed, and if you follow it until it meets RI 165, you will hike almost 4 miles one way.

The Breakheart Pond Trail—To reach the Breakheart Pond Trail, follow RI 165 west from the RI 3 intersection for 2.9 miles to the unpaved Frosty Hollow Road. Continue north on Frosty Hollow Road for 1.4 miles until you can go no farther; turn right and proceed .5 mile to Breakheart Pond. Park at the parking area near the pond. The Breakheart Pond Trail is also blazed in yellow, and if you follow this trail it will lead you in a big loop to Penny Hill and back to the parking area, about a 6-mile walk.

The Escoheag Trail—To reach the Escoheag Trail, follow RI 165 west from the RI 3 intersection 5.3 miles to Escoheag Hill Road. Turn right and follow this road .9 mile until you reach Austin Farm Road. Turn right onto this road and, bearing left, follow it .4 mile to the Escoheag Trail. This trail is blazed in white, and if you follow it to the Falls River and back you will hike approximately 3 miles.

The Beach Pond Trail—To reach the Beach Pond Trail, follow RI 165 west 7.7 miles past the RI 3 intersection to the Beach Pond parking area on your right. The Yellow trail starts on the other side of the road, and by following this trail to the Connecticut border and back you will hike approximately 3.5 miles.

BIRDING:

Because Arcadia is such a large tract of preserved land, it offers the Rhode Island bird-watcher the greatest variety of habitats in one refuge—immense Hemlock forests, White Pine forests, deciduous woodlands, fields, large ponds and lakes, and an abundance of woodland streams—through which to search for birds. In the summer you may see many hikers and dirt-bikers, but do not get discouraged; there are still many species of birds to be seen here.

Four of the most notable Arcadia breeders are Red-breasted Nuthatch, Solitary Vireo, Whip-poor-will, and Nashville Warbler. These species can all be found with relative ease in the spring and summer just by listening for their distinctive calls, although the Whip-poor-will usually calls only at dusk or late in the evening. Some of the other breeders that should be looked for include Black-billed and Yellow-billed Cuckoos, Northern Bobwhite, Northern and Louisiana Waterthrushes, Scarlet Tanager, and Red-bellied Woodpecker.

As you walk through these woods, you should be attuned to the sounds of Rose-breasted Grosbeaks, Black-and-white Warblers, Tree Swallows, Great Crested Flycatchers, Blue-gray Gnatcatchers, Veeries, and Hermit Thrushes. You should also pay attention to any rustlings that you hear on the ground. Try to see which bird is making the noise (it's not always a Gray Squirrel!). Sometimes the sound is made by Brown Thrashers or Ovenbirds, but it could be caused by the scratching feet of a Ruffed Grouse, Wild Turkey, or Rufous-sided Towhee.

Eastern Kingbird

You should investigate any movement that you see in the treetops, for you may catch a glimpse of a Northern Oriole, Scarlet Tanager, Least Flycatcher, or Yellow-throated Vireo. Also, Blue-winged Warbler, Red-eyed Vireo, and Pine Warbler might be seen. Along the woodland streams you may be fortunate enough to see one of the many woodland species taking a bath as they all must do. You may even see a Louisiana Waterthrush hunting for insects along the waterway. If you listen closely, you may hear the springtime hammering of woodpeckers proclaiming territory. Downy and Hairy Woodpeckers are the most common here, but Red-headed and Pileated (probably breeding here) have also been seen.

During migration, these woodlands can seem to overflow with migrant land birds; Blackpoll, Tennessee, Bay-breasted, Canada, Worm-eating, and Mourning Warblers have all been seen here. Solitary and Philadelphia Vireos and Yellow-bellied and Acadian Flycatchers also have been seen passing through. You should also look for returning Ruby-throated Hummingbirds feeding on the first available flowers.

In the winter these woodlands are much less active. However, this area has proved itself in the past to be one of the most productive owling spots in the state. In late winter when all of the Rhode Island breeding owls are at least thinking about setting up territories, a nighttime stroll through this area will often reward you with the calls of Great Horned Owls (begin calling regularly as early as January), Barred Owls (regularly heard in March), or Eastern Screech-Owls (seem to answer year-round). December, January, and February are the best months to find northern wintering species. If you search the pine groves thoroughly during the day, you may be fortunate enough to see a Long-eared Owl or even a tiny Northern Saw-whet Owl hiding from the intense daylight and the watchful eyes of mobbing Black-capped Chickadees. Other interesting wintering species that have been found here are Pine Siskins, Red- and White-winged Crossbills, and Common Redpolls, all of which can be easy to see or hear one winter and almost impossible to find the next.

14

Norman Bird Sanctuary

▼

Specialties: Breeding Birds, Migrants

S.***, Su. ***, F.**, W.*

▼

The Norman Bird Sanctuary, a privately owned wildlife refuge, is probably the one site I would recommend to a birder who wants to do some summer birding in Rhode Island. It seems to be one of the few areas in the state where you can beat the summer-birding blahs by finding good birds even at this time of year.

The birding can be fine at other times, too. On some days, particularly during migration, you may encounter almost 50 species of land birds passing through the deciduous forests and the fields here.

It is also one of the easiest places in the state to find Ruby-throated Hummingbirds; they nest in trees along the edges of most of the fields, feeding on the nectar of the abundant wildflowers. And there are saltwater marshes you can look over, as well as a freshwater pond at the center of the refuge.

Norman Bird Sanctuary has a small museum you can visit. Injured raptors are kept behind the headquarters building.

This is the only birding area mentioned in this book that requires an entrance fee at all times of the year. The general admittance fee is $2 per person. The sanctuary is open daily from 9 A.M. to 5 P.M. year-round.

DIRECTIONS:

From the north, take RI 138 (East Main Road) south to RI 138A (Aquidneck Avenue). Follow that road south until you

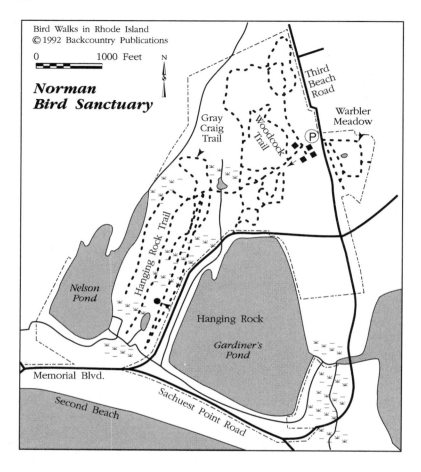

Bird Walks in Rhode Island
© 1992 Backcountry Publications

0   1000 Feet   N

**Norman
Bird Sanctuary**

reach the Atlantic Ocean. Turn left onto Sachuest Point Road
and proceed for approximately 1.7 miles to Gardiner's Pond
on your left. Turn left just before the pond (the road you
would use if you were going to bird Gardiner's Pond) and
follow this road to Third Beach Road (1 mile). Turn left onto
Third Beach Road and proceed less than .5 mile to the Norman
Bird Sanctuary on your left. Park in the area provided.

From the west, follow RI 138 east over the Newport
Bridge. After crossing the bridge, turn left at the first traffic

light and follow this road for 2.8 miles through four traffic
lights. Turn right onto Third Beach Road at the Norman Bird
Sanctuary sign (partly obscured by tree branches). Follow this
road south for .7 mile to the sanctuary on your right.

BIRDING:

During the lengthened days of spring, summer, and fall, the
best times to bird-watch are from 5 A.M. to 10 A.M. and 4 P.M.
to 7:30 P.M. Unfortunately, the sanctuary is not open throughout these periods, so it makes sense to spend the morning
birding elsewhere and come to this sanctuary during the
afternoon. Midday birding is usually much less productive
than morning or late afternoon because of the hot sun; however, if you are willing to work at it, you can still find
interesting birds.

After parking, you can walk behind the headquarters
building to view the injured raptors. As you begin walking
behind the cage area, one of the first trails that you come across
will be the Woodcock Trail on your right. This trail encom-

Ruby-throated Hummingbird

passes a large field that is managed so as to attract breeding American Woodcocks. There is another trail a bit farther down on your left that, during the spring and summer, also harbors woodcocks. Ring-necked Pheasants, Ruby-throated Hummingbirds, Tree and Barn Swallows, and even Purple Martins can be seen in or above this field as well.

The trails through the Norman Bird Sanctuary will bring you through some excellent habitat for woodland birds. On one walk through these woods I had the great delight of seeing both the Black-billed and Yellow-billed Cuckoos perched in the same tree. In the summer these woods also abound with several species of warblers and vireos. The Red-eyed Vireo is the most common vireo seen here, but Yellow-throated and Warbling Vireos can also be found. Black-and-white Warblers, Common Yellowthroats, Blue-winged Warblers, and American Redstarts are all common here in the spring and summer.

During migration, the haunting songs of Veery, Hermit Thrush, Wood Thrush and sometimes Swainson's Thrush can be heard echoing through the forest on a good day. Nelson Pond at the center of the refuge is one of the best places to look for migrating land birds; they are sometimes common as they feed on the insects that abound by the water's edge. Least Flycatcher, Northern Waterthrush, Canada Warbler, and Winter Wren are species of particular interest to look for.

If you follow the Gray Craig Trail, you will be led to a spectacular view of the Gray Craig Pond. During migration, migrating waterfowl such as Blue-winged Teal, Northern Shoveler, Ruddy Duck, and Ring-necked Duck can sometimes be found here. Another trail, the Hanging Rock Trail, will afford you a view of a very nice marsh. When the water is low in this area, shorebirds and herons will occasionally gather here to feed, and you may even see an American Bittern skulking around the water's edge.

One last area that you should visit before you leave is the Warbler Meadow. You can reach this meadow by returning to the parking lot and walking directly across Third Beach Road. This spot can provide very good birding. Many species have been seen here, including Wilson's, Bay-breasted, Chestnut-sided, and Hooded Warblers.

15

Carolina Management Area

▼

Specialties: Migrant Land Birds

S.**, Su.**, F.**, W.*

▼

The Carolina Management Area is an extensive, rugged hiking and hunting area owned by the state of Rhode Island. Except for White Brook Pond, the birding here is often somewhat slow. However, there are a number of interesting species to be seen. I think perhaps that this area is best for those birders who enjoy long hikes and like to study the common birds as well as look for uncommon ones.

DIRECTIONS:

From the north, follow I-95 south from Providence to Exit 3A, "RI 138 east." Continue on RI 138 east for approximately 2.1 miles to RI 112 south. Proceed south on RI 112 to Pine Hill Road. Turn right and follow this road .7 mile to a small bridge over a feeder river for White Brook Pond. The parking area for the trails is another 1.3 miles west on Pine Hill Road near the brown building on your left.

From the west, drive north from the Connecticut border on I-95 to Exit 3A, "RI 138 east," and proceed as above.

The first stop in the Carolina Management Area is White Brook Pond. This pond can be difficult to see from the road, but it is well worth the effort. To say that White Brook is one of the best waterfowl locations in the state would almost be an understatement. Species that gather here in the late fall include Green-winged and Blue-winged Teals, Northern Shovelers

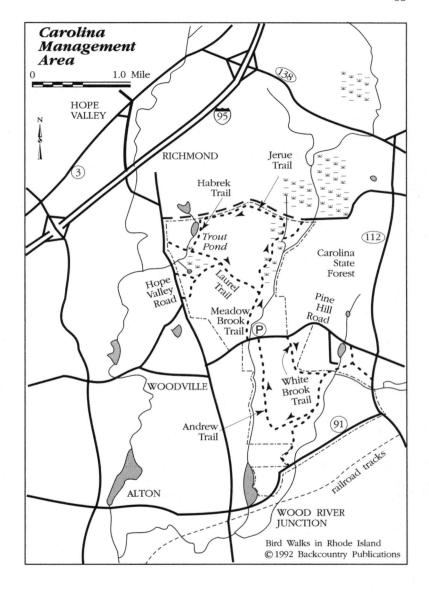

Carolina
Management
Area

0   1.0 Mile

HOPE
VALLEY

N

138

95

RICHMOND

3

Jerue
Trail

Habrek
Trail

Trout
Pond

112

Carolina
State
Forest

Hope
Valley
Road

Laurel
Trail

Meadow
Brook
Trail

P

Pine
Hill
Road

WOODVILLE

White
Brook
Trail

Andrew
Trail

91

ALTON

railroad tracks

WOOD RIVER
JUNCTION

Bird Walks in Rhode Island
© 1992 Backcountry Publications

Evening Grosbeak

(small numbers), Gadwall, Ring-necked Duck, and occasionally a migrant Tundra Swan.

From the parking area near the brown building you can
follow one of two different trails. To walk the southern
portion of the management area, walk back (east) along Pine
Hill Road for .3 mile to the White Brook Trail on your right.
Walk south along this trail to the Pawcatuck River, turn right,
and follow the river for .2 mile to the Andrew Trail, and turn
right again to follow the Andrew Trail back to the parking
area. This whole walk is less than 3 miles. To walk the
northern portion of the management area, walk west along
Pine Hill Road, where after .1 mile (just over the stream, which
is called Meadow Brook) you will see the Meadow Brook Trail
on your right. Walk north on the Meadow Brook Trail for
approximately .7 mile to the Jerue Trail on your left; follow
the Jerue Trail for .5 mile to the Habrek Trail. The Habrek
Trail is also on your left and will lead you to the Laurel Trail,
which will bring you back to Pine Hill Road. Turn left on Pine
Hill Road and walk approximately .5 mile to the parking area.
This walk is just over 3.5 miles. A word of caution, though;
Carolina Management Area is very large and can be confusing

to someone unfamiliar with its trails; it may be best to walk through the area for the first time with someone who knows the trails.

BIRDING:

If you decide to hike along the White Brook Trail, you will quickly find yourself in a thick white pine forest. In the spring, summer, and fall some of the species that you can expect to see in a forest of this type are Pine Warbler, White-breasted Nuthatch, Ruby-crowned Kinglet, Wood Thrush, Black-throated Green Warbler, Yellow-rumped Warbler, Ovenbird, and Downy and Hairy Woodpeckers. The White Brook Trail will bring you to the Pawcatuck River. If you cross the river you are no longer on state land, so it is best to stay on the north side of the river. You should, however, check the river and the thickets along its bank for species such as Yellow Warbler and Common Yellowthroat. At some point along your walk you will probably flush a Green-backed Heron from the water's edge. You should also look for bathing birds—all birds must bathe whether it is in the water like most species or in the dust like House Sparrows, and it is not altogether uncommon to see several species engaged in this activity at the same time.

The White Brook Trail also brings you through some cornfields. These fields should be checked for Eastern Bluebirds and Tree Swallows, not to mention Wild Turkeys feeding on the fallen corn.

If you decide to follow the northern trails, you will find yourself in an area filled with trails, crossroads, and a variety of habitats. If the gates are open (usually only during the hunting season, so be careful!) and you do not feel up to a hike, you can drive a good portion of the northern trails, but as a birder I do recommend that you walk these trails; birding is much easier without the noise and inconvenience of an auto.

On the northern trails the woodlands are a mixture of deciduous, White Pine, Pitch Pine, Red Pine, and scrubby habitats, each of which can harbor an interesting array of species. Carolina Management Area is host to several breeding birds of note, Red-shouldered Hawk, Black-throated Green Warbler, Red-breasted Nuthatch, Northern Goshawk, and Ruffed Grouse. The Red-breasted Nuthatch and Black-throated Green Warbler are easy to locate because of their distinctive calls, but the Northern Goshawk and the Ruffed Grouse are species that you almost have to stumble over to see. (The Ruffed Grouse can be difficult to flush, and the Northern Goshawk is usually aware of your presence long before you are aware of his.) On the forest floor you may see Ovenbird, Brown Thrasher (becoming harder to find), and Wood Thrush. In the thickets you can probably agitate a House Wren so much that it will pop into view.

During migration many species of migrants pass through these woodlands. By early to mid-April the songs of Pine and Prairie Warblers can be heard, as well as the occasional call of the Yellow-bellied Sapsucker and the rough call of the Eastern Phoebe. However, by the time mid-May arrives these woodlands echo with the calls and songs of perhaps 40 or 50 different species, some of them proclaiming territory and others simply passing through.

The best time to identify most Rhode Island birds easily is during the spring migration. During this time almost all of the birds are singing their characteristic songs and all are sporting their distinctive breeding plumages, whereas when late summer and fall arrive most birds are silent and molting into dull winter colors. Another problem with fall bird identification is that you have many immature birds to identify; even though they are in fresh plumages, these often look wholly different from any of the adult plumages.

After the thrills of the spring and fall migrations are over, winter birding away from the coast can often be very boring. However, if you are interested in becoming more familiar with Rhode Island's permanent residents, winter is the best time. Downy and Hairy Woodpeckers are easily found, as well as Black-capped Chickadees and Tufted Titmice. Our winter residents are also easy to find; these include Tree Sparrows, White-throated Sparrows, and those late-winter visitors, Fox Sparrows. If you are particularly lucky, you may even find a Long-eared Owl or a very rare Black-backed Woodpecker (one record for this location).

16

Succotash Marsh

▼

Specialties: Waders, Shorebirds

S.**, Su.**, F.**, W.**

▼

If you enjoy birding the coastal salt marshes and mud flats as I do, then you'll appreciate the Succotash Marsh. When the tide waters are low, many species of shorebirds and waders can be found here, particularly in the spring and fall. The drive around the marsh is a simple loop from US 1 to Snug Harbor, but for a bird-watcher it can be very exciting. You may even be lucky enough to have a Snowy Owl fly over your car on a cool winter day.

DIRECTIONS:

From the north, follow I-95 south from Providence for 13.5 miles to RI 4 south, Exit 9, "North Kingstown." RI 4 south becomes US 1 south after about 6.5 miles. Follow US 1 south for approximately 14.8 miles to "Jerusalem, Snug Harbor" exit. Continue on this road (Succotash Road) for .8 mile to the Succotash Marsh on your left. The road that leads around the marsh is long and the marsh itself very large, so it is best simply to drive along this road and scan the marsh for birds.

From the west: Exit 1 off I-95 will put you on RI 3 south. Follow RI 3 south until it intersects RI 216 (1.7 miles), then follow RI 216 south for approximately 6.4 miles to US 1. After turning left onto US 1 (north), follow this road for 10.8 miles to the "Jerusalem, Snug Harbor" exit and proceed as above.

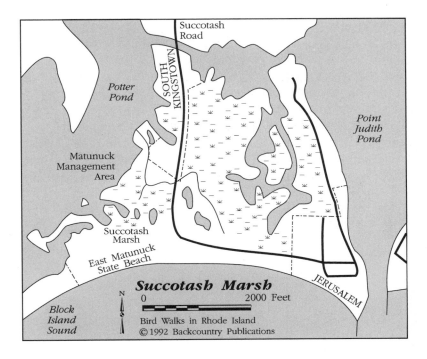

Succotash Marsh

0   2000 Feet

Bird Walks in Rhode Island
© 1992 Backcountry Publications

BIRDING:

When the tide levels are low, during migration this marsh can sometimes harbor a vast array of shorebird species; some of the more common species to be seen are Least and Semipalmated Sandpipers, Short-billed Dowitchers, and Semipalmated Plovers. Other shorebirds that you may see are Greater and Lesser Yellowlegs, Black-bellied Plovers, and Stilt Sandpipers. Ruff has even been seen here!

Waders can often be found in this marsh—usually large numbers occur in the fall. Great Egrets, Snowy Egrets, Little Blue Herons, Glossy Ibis, and Great Blue Herons are the species most frequently seen. Flocks of migrating waterfowl can be impressive as they gather here in the spring and fall. Black Ducks are common migrants along with Common

Mergansers and Buffleheads. You should also check for Green-winged Teals, Blue-winged Teals, and Gadwalls.

If you are lucky, you may see one of the few American Bitterns that invariably pass through this marsh. You should also look for species such as Clapper Rail (usually in the taller salt-marsh grasses) and Common Snipe. If you are really lucky, you may see a King Rail. Although the King Rail is very rare in salt marshes, hybrids between this rail and the Clapper Rail are sometimes found. In fact, in 1976 two Rhode Island birders found a mixed breeding pair of Clapper and King Rail.

In the summer the beach traffic from the nearby East Matunuck State Beach is usually enough to keep the rails away, but certain die-hard species like the Sharp-tailed Sparrow and the Seaside Sparrow can still be found here amid the confusion of sun-tanners and loose dogs. Some of the other

Glossy Ibis

Succotash Marsh

summer residents which you are likely to see include Red-winged Blackbirds, Common Grackles, and Green-backed Herons.

Wintertime in this salt marsh is not a time of scarce birds, but rather a time when different birds can be found. The tidal movement of water in and out of the marsh keeps the water mostly unfrozen. Because of this, large groups of wintering waterfowl can be found here, including Black Ducks, Red-breasted Mergansers, Buffleheads, and less common winterers such as Northern Pintails and Green-winged Teals. This marsh also seems to be one of the favored wintering areas of Great Blue Herons. Coastal marshes are also the winter home to species such as Short-eared Owl, which is usually seen hunting over the marsh only at dawn and dusk; even an occasional Snowy Owl is sighted here.

If it is wintertime, you should not leave without checking the East Matunuck State Beach parking area, which is one of the best places in the state to see Snow Buntings, Horned Larks, and the rare Lapland Longspur; all three of these species like the gravelly surface. A quick walk over the small sand dune to the beach will give you a fine view of the ocean, and from here you can look for the many sea duck species that winter in Rhode Island. If you are here during the months of October and November, you should look for late Palm Warblers—these warblers seem to love the coastal beaches as they • migrate southward. They are easy to spot while they walk the beach, bobbing their tails incessantly and thus showing the only bright color they wear in the fall: their conspicuous yellow under-tail coverts.

17

Buck Hill Management Area

▼

Specialties: Breeders, Winter Finches

S.**, Su.***, F.**, W.***

▼

Located in the extreme northwest corner of the state, the Buck Hill Management Area is a very extensive and somewhat isolated birding area. Good birds can be found at Buck Hill, particularly in the wintertime. The trails can be downright confusing—if you are unfamiliar with this area, follow the directions as closely as possible to avoid getting lost. Once you have hiked here a few times, you can begin to explore new trails and will undoubtedly find new birding areas. Plan to spend considerable time here, for the hiking trails are quite long.

DIRECTIONS:

From the north, follow I-295 south to exit 7B, "Greenville, US 44 west." Continue west on US 44 for approximately 8 miles to RI 102 north. RI 102 north and RI 100 join for a short distance at this point. Follow RI 100 north for 6.8 miles to Buck Hill Road on your left. Turn left onto Buck Hill Road and proceed for 2.3 miles to an unmarked access road on your right. Follow this dirt road for .3 mile to the parking lot.

From the west, I-95 north will bring you to I-295 north (exit 11). Follow I-295 north to exit 7B, "Greenville, US 44 west," and drive west on US 44 for 8 miles to the RI 102 intersection. Proceed as above.

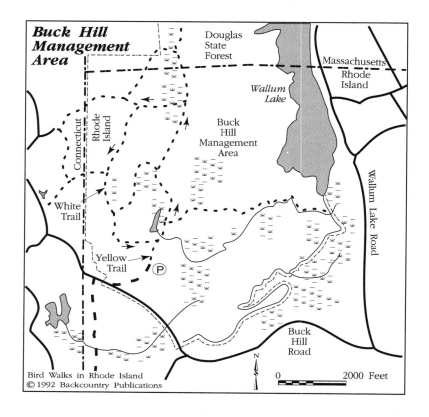

The walk that I most frequently use is the same walk outlined in Ken Weber's *Walks and Rambles in Rhode Island*. From the parking area follow the dirt road north (Yellow Trail) for approximately 1.4 miles to an old woods road crossing your path—this road is lined with stone walls and is unmistakable. Turn left onto this road and walk about .5 mile to a grassy trail on your left. This trail will turn sharply right after a short distance; you will want to continue straight onto a narrow footpath that is at first difficult to see. The footpath soon intersects the White Trail, which will bring you back to the parking area. The entire walk is roughly 3.5 miles.

BIRDING:

There are many small ponds along the trails in the Buck Hill Management Area, and each is equipped with its own Wood Duck nesting box; therefore, from mid-April through the summer these attractive and shy little ducks are common here. The woodland ponds are also rich in insect life, so it is not unusual to find a vast number of insect-eating birds here, such as Tree Swallows, Eastern Kingbirds, and Yellow Warblers.

Shortly after you leave the parking area, you will come to a large pond that was created when a brook was dammed to flood a surrounding forest. There are many dead trees standing throughout this pond, and you may find many woodpeckers and Tree Swallows taking advantage of the soft wood and nesting here. Furthermore, wooded swamps provide a good area to search for the elusive Pileated Woodpecker. If one is present, you'll hear its loud chattering call and almost thunder-like hammering. Another species that prefers the wooded swamp is the Barred Owl; you may be fortunate enough to find one of these large owls staring down at you from an exposed perch.

Other interesting birds that you may see here are Eastern Bluebirds, feeding in the grassy fields; House Wrens, calling from the thick undergrowth; and Brown Thrashers, Prairie Warblers, Field Sparrows, Chipping Sparrows, and Wood Thrushes—not to mention the hearty populations of Veeries, Scarlet Tanagers, Red-eyed Vireos, Black-billed Cuckoos, and Northern Bobwhites which can be heard in the spring and summer. These woodlands are also home to a few sought-after birds such as the Northern Goshawk, Red-shouldered Hawk, and Whip-poor-will. All three of these birds can be rather difficult to see, but with a little perseverance and luck you will sometimes find them.

In the late summer you can still hear the songs of some of

The start of the trail at Buck Hill Management Area

the late-nesting species. The buzzy trills of the Cedar Wax-wing, the flute-like song of the Rose-breasted Grosbeak (more often you hear the "squeaky-door" call note of this species), and the familiar chips of the American Goldfinch can be heard easily in July and August.

Migration is a time to look for interesting birds at this refuge. Because of the extensive uncleared forests, many migrant land birds find ample food supplies here. Transients that have been seen here include Canada, Bay-breasted, and Black-poll Warblers, Solitary and Yellow-throated Vireos, and occasional Yellow-bellied and Acadian Flycatchers.

After all of the migrants have passed through on their way south and the cold weather moves in, the time to search for winter visitors has arrived. The Buck Hill Management Area and the Wallum Lake area are probably the most reliable places in the state to look for winter finches. Species to look for include Purple Finches, permanent residents which breed here; Evening Grosbeaks, fairly regular winter visitors; Red Crossbills, always uncommon in Rhode Island; White-winged Crossbills, which seem to occur more frequently than Red Crossbills; and Common Redpolls and Pine Siskins, each of which can be somewhat common in some years and absent in others. Even Pine Grosbeaks have been seen here foraging with the other winter finches.

Winter birding at Buck Hill will also undoubtedly produce Ruffed Grouse and occasionally Wild Turkey.

18

Beavertail Point Park

▼

Specialties: Migrant Hawks, Sea Ducks

S.**, Su.**, F.***, W.***

▼

Beavertail Point Park can be a very exciting coastal birding area. This park's location at the extreme southern tip of Conanicut Island (Jamestown) places it in perfect position to play host to a number of wintering waterfowl species as well as occasional alcid and seabird species. A trip to this park in the early morning on a winter day, particularly after a night of heavy winds, could produce any one of a number of interesting species.

DIRECTIONS:

From the north, follow I-95 south from Providence for 13.5 miles to RI 4 south, Exit 9, "North Kingstown." RI 4 south becomes US 1 south after about 6.5 miles. Follow US 1 south to RI 138 east—this will bring you to the Jamestown Bridge. After crossing the Jamestown Bridge, continue east .7 mile until you reach a traffic light. Turn right at this light and continue for 2 miles to another traffic light. Proceed straight through this light for 3.2 miles on Beavertail Road until you reach the park. There is one parking lot on the east side of the peninsula after you enter the park and another on the west side past the lighthouse. I recommend parking after the lighthouse because it affords easier access to the oceanfront.

From the west, follow I-95 north to Exit 3A, "RI 138 east." Continue on RI 138 east to the Jamestown Bridge and proceed as above.

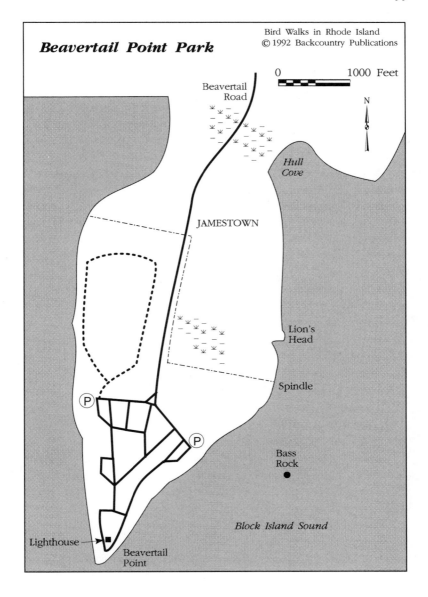

Bird Walks in Rhode Island
© 1992 Backcountry Publications

Beavertail Point Park

0   1000 Feet

N

Beavertail
Road

Hull
Cove

JAMESTOWN

Lion's
Head

Spindle

P

P

Bass
Rock

Block Island Sound

Lighthouse

Beavertail
Point

BIRDING:

Beavertail Point is best birded in the fall and winter. In the winter you can usually find abundant sea ducks off the coast, and in the fall many migrants may pass through the thickets of this park, hiding from the hawks that can often be seen passing overhead.

Winter birding at Beavertail mainly produces such species as the large and bulky-looking Common Loon, and the always common winter sea duck: the Red-breasted Merganser. Other birds that you will probably see are Common Goldeneye, Red-throated Loon, Horned Grebe, Red-necked Grebe, and occasionally a Harlequin Duck or a Barrow's Goldeneye. If you search the rocky coastline of this park, you can often see Purple Sandpipers, and in the fall you may even see Ruddy Turnstones and Spotted Sandpipers hopping from rock to rock searching for a marine meal or an American Oystercatcher foraging on the mussel-covered rocks with its immense reddish-orange bill.

Also, alcids are occasional winter visitors to this coastal area. After large winter storms which push many pelagic birds into the coastal waters, Razorbills and Dovekies have been seen feeding here. Even Black Guillemots have been seen sitting on the rocks resting after cold winter storms.

In November the Northern Gannet migration really gets into full swing, and Beavertail is a great place to see these spectacular birds as they glide high over the water on long, black-tipped, white wings.

These birds can be seen occasionally offshore throughout the winter, but it is not until mid-March that they begin to move northward in considerable numbers again. Sometimes in late March a Manx Shearwater is seen mingling with the gannets. Although this is an uncommon sight, the possibility of seeing one from shore is enough to interest almost any birder.

The fall migration at Beavertail can be very exhilarating. Many times I have traveled to this park on a cool September morning to witness the streams of migrating hawks that frequently pass over when the weather conditions are optimal. When the weather is cold and northwest winds prevail, most migrants are stimulated into making the journey southward. (I don't think anyone would argue against a cold morning being an extra "kicker" for birds, although true migratory behavior is related to the photoperiod—that is, length of day; for example, longer days in the spring stimulate migratory species to migrate north.)

Some of the hawks commonly seen here in the fall are Sharp-shinned Hawks, with their characteristic three-flaps-and-a-glide flight; Cooper's Hawks (uncommon), with a flight pattern similar to that of a Sharp-shinned but slower; and Northern Harriers, with their characteristic uptilted wings. American Kestrels are also common migrants here, and you may see a few Merlins and Peregrine Falcons as well. Other species to look for if you catch a good flight are Ospreys, Turkey Vultures, Bald Eagles, Broad-winged Hawks, and large wandering flocks of Blue Jays.

American Oystercatcher

The lighthouse at Beavertail Point

After a foggy night in September or May, you may be
fortunate enough to find large numbers of migrant land birds
that were forced down by the inclement weather. It is not
uncommon to discover many different species concentrated in
a favorable location after one of these nights. Because of this,
poor-weather birding can be the best, and coastal areas such
as Beavertail Point are the best places to look if you want to
find one of these large, mixed-species groups.

19

George Washington Management Area

▼

Specialties: Land Birds

S.**, Su.**, F.**, W.**

▼

If you are looking for a birding area in Rhode Island where you can do some upland birding as well as some camping, the George Washington Management Area offers both. But because pines are predominant here, summer birding can be somewhat slow; you will probably have much more fun camping than birding. Winter birding, however, is usually exciting, and you can make day trips to this area to look for owls as well as winter finches.

DIRECTIONS:

From the north, follow I-295 south to exit 7B, "Greenville, US 44 west." Continue west on US 44, through a number of intersections and route junctions, for approximately 13.3 miles to the entrance on the right to the George Washington camping area. The dirt road that takes you through the camping area will also bring you to Casimer Pulaski Memorial State Park. Another way to reach Pulaski Park is to continue past the camping area entrance on US 44 for 1.8 more miles to the Casimir Pulaski Memorial State Park sign on the right; turn right here and follow the road for .8 mile to the park parking area.

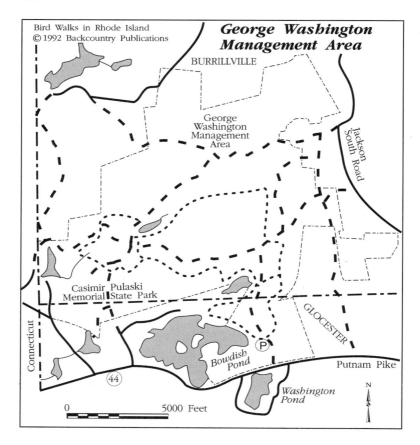

Bird Walks in Rhode Island
© 1992 Backcountry Publications

George Washington Management Area

BURRILLVILLE

George Washington Management Area

Jackson South Road

Casimir Pulaski Memorial State Park

Connecticut

Bowdish Pond

44

Putnam Pike

Washington Pond

GLOCESTER

N

0   5000 Feet

From the west, I-95 north will bring you to I-295 north (exit 11). Follow I-295 north to Exit 7B, "Greenville, US 44 west," and proceed as above.

BIRDING:

The George Washington Management Area, including the contiguous Casimir Pulaski Memorial State Park, is a very extensive tract of state-owned land that is laced with crossroads and trails. The best way to bird this area is to walk or drive along the camping area road and turn off it when you find a trail that you want to explore.

The dominant type of tree cover found here is the Eastern Hemlock; these are beautiful evergreen trees that provide a cool, moist woodland through which to search for birds. Species to look for are Northern Waterthrush, Veery, Hermit Thrush, Ovenbird, Golden-crowned Kinglet, and Black-throated Green and Pine Warblers. The large cone crops that these trees often produce provide a suitable food source for the flocks of Tufted Titmice and Black-capped Chickadees that roam through these woodlands.

There is a big tract of deciduous forest toward the northern end of the camping area. The oaks and maples can attract many different species of warblers during the spring and fall migrations. Chestnut-sided, Blackburnian, Blackpoll, Black-throated Blue, and Prairie Warblers can all be found here as they pick insects off the branches and leaves. Warblers which have appeared with great regularity are Mourning Warbler, Canada Warbler, Black-throated Green Warbler, and Pine Warbler—although the latter two will be found almost exclusively in the conifers.

In the summer you should concentrate your attention on the deciduous trees and look for such species as the Scarlet Tanager, Northern Oriole, and Yellow-throated Vireo, as well as Red-eyed Vireo and Black-and-white Warbler. If you travel enough of this area, you will come upon one of the large ponds. You should look for Tree Swallows catching insects over the water's surface and listen for the cheerful chattering of Chimney Swifts as they catch insects high overhead. Also, if you are here at dusk look for the flocks of Chimney Swifts, to be followed later at night by small groups of Common Nighthawks (particularly in September). The pond at Casimir Pulaski Memorial State Park is the best place to see the swallows, swifts, and nighthawks.

Interestingly, Casimir Pulaski Memorial State Park is one of the few Rhode Island locations where Northern Saw-whet

Owls are suspected of breeding. These tiny owls are difficult to see, partly because of their small size and partly because they do not reveal their location by flushing easily; in fact, sometimes you can almost reach out and grab one of these little owls before it will try to escape. They are usually easier to see in the wintertime because then they do not roost in tree cavities.

Red-shouldered Hawks, Whip-poor-wills, and Pine Warblers are among the notable breeding birds of the George Washington Management Area.

20

Lincoln Woods State Park

▼

Specialties: Migrant Land Birds

S.***, Su.**, F.***, W.*

▼

Located just north of the capital city of Providence, Lincoln Woods State Park is a haven for people trapped in the city as well as for birders. The best birding done at Lincoln Woods is usually done in the morning, particularly during migration when many different species of land birds are passing through the state. If you choose to visit on some early morning during migration, you will probably come across some other birders as well as walkers and joggers. The birds do not seem to mind all of the people in the park, so you should not be discouraged either.

DIRECTIONS:

From the north, follow I-95 south to Exit 23, "Charles Street, RI 146." Turn right off this exit and follow this road for .1 mile to RI 146 north. Continue north on RI 146 to the "Lincoln Woods State Park" exit. Turn left off the exit and drive .3 mile to the park. You can park in one of the available lots after entering.

From the west, follow I-95 north to Exit 23, "Lincoln, State Offices." Bear left at this dual exit (to Lincoln), and drive north on RI 146 to the "Lincoln Woods State Park" exit. Proceed as above.

Red-Headed
Woodpecker

BIRDING:

The best way to bird the Lincoln Woods State Park is to follow the trails that surround Olney Pond. Because of the pond's large size and the surrounding woodlands, this area can be most inviting to migrant land birds and waterfowl (if not just to walkers, bikers, and joggers). The best time is between the hours of 5:30 A.M. and 7:30 A.M. from about late April to mid-May in the spring and late August to early November in the fall. If you can bring yourself to bird this early in the morning (as most birders can), you will sometimes find many interesting species.

Some of the warblers that you should look for during migration are Black-throated Blue, Magnolia, Blackburnian, Black-throated Green, Pine, Prairie, Palm (spring only for inland locations), Tennessee, Nashville, Blue-winged, and Yellow-rumped Warblers. Migrant Vireos, too, can be found here: White-eyed, Warbling, and Solitary are not uncommon. You might see two of eastern North America's largest flycatchers; Eastern Kingbird with its distinctive trilling call is common around the water's edge, and Great Crested Flycatcher can usually be located in the denser areas of the woods.

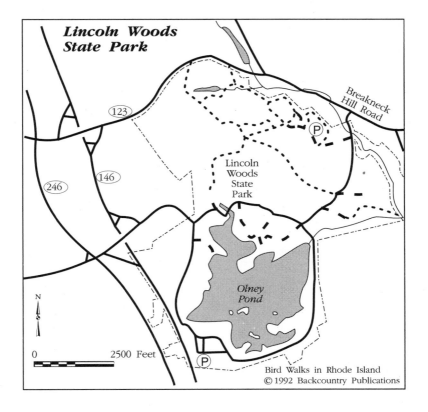

Waterfowl can be found here, particularly in the fall. Be sure to check the many little coves and islands of Olney Pond for Wood Ducks, Hooded Mergansers, Ring-necked Ducks, and (rarely) Blue-winged Teals. Also, look for the Green-backed and Great Blue Herons that frequent this pond.

Woodland birding in the fall can be one of the most challenging quests for a birder, for it is at this time that the migrant warblers are wearing only a drab reminder of their brilliant spring plumages. What this means is that many of the bright yellow and black which you saw only a few months ago are now replaced by dull olive and white. Some of the easier warblers to identify in the fall are Black-and-white Warbler, with little or no change from spring; Prairie Warbler, which still retains some of its facial markings; and Common Yellowthroat, on which the yellow throat is relatively obvious in all plumages. However, such species as Bay-breasted Warbler, Blackpoll Warbler, and Tennessee Warbler can all be so plain-looking in fall plumage that positive identification can often be difficult until the bird is seen very clearly.

21

Swan Point Cemetery

▼

Specialties: Migrant Land Birds

S.***, Su.*, F.***, W.**

▼

Located on the east side of Providence along the Seekonk River, Swan Point Cemetery is probably the best place in the state to witness the spring land bird migration, much as Block Island is the best place to witness the fall migration. More species pass through this cemetery and are seen by more birders than anywhere else in the state. From Cape May Warblers to Lincoln's Sparrows and Caspian Terns, this cemetery certainly has the potential to add many new species to any birder's list.

Bordered on all sides by civilization, it is an oasis of trees, insects, and running water which provide tired migrating birds with all of the essentials for continuing their migration northward. Warblers, thrushes, flycatchers, and sparrows abound, and for this reason hordes of enthusiastic bird-watchers come here in early May, hoping to find a rare Kentucky Warbler or Golden-winged Warbler.

DIRECTIONS:

From the north, follow I-95 south to Exit 24, "Branch Avenue." Turn left off the exit and proceed on Branch Avenue (east) to North Main Street. Turn left onto North Main Street and follow this road .4 mile to Rochambeau Avenue (first traffic light), turn right up a steep hill, and continue across Hope Street .7 mile to Elmgrove Avenue. Turn left at Elmgrove

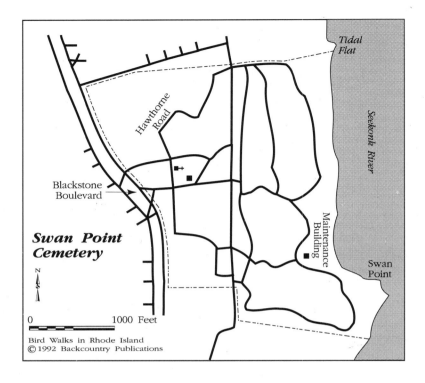

Avenue and follow this road for .4 mile to Blackstone Boulevard to the main entrance to Swan Point Cemetery.

From the west, follow I-95 north to Exit 23, "Branch Avenue," and turn right off the exit. Continue .1 mile to North Main Street and proceed as above.

BIRDING:

Swan Point can be referred to as an island habitat—that is, a large section of woodland habitat isolated from other similar habitats by the surrounding city. Consequently, most of the migrant land birds in the area have no choice other than to spend the day feeding at this cemetery. This is good news for birders because it means that large concentrations of many

different species can be found during peak migration; therefore, in spring the birding at Swan Point can be outstanding,
especially following a night of southwest winds.

After parking either on Blackstone Boulevard or in the
cemetery in one of the designated areas, the first and probably
best area to bird is the extensively wooded area off Hawthorn
Road. You can reach this road by turning left after entering
through the main gate and turning left onto your first road.
This small forest is crisscrossed with trails to provide access to
almost any part. In fact, these trails are often the ones used by
the leaders of the Swan Point bird walks, sponsored each May
by the Audubon Society of Rhode Island.

This section of woodland is composed of various species
of trees, including Oaks, Maples, and Beeches as well as
Birches and conifers. Such variety aids the birder by providing
suitable habitats for many different species of birds.

Warblers to look and listen for in this forested area in early
May include Blackburnian, Yellow-rumped, Northern
Parula, American Redstart, and Black-throated Green Warblers. Some of the less common species that are fairly regular
in spring are Mourning (late May/early June), Canada, Cerulean, Hooded, Wilson's and occasionally Kentucky, Orange-
crowned, Prothonotary and Yellow-throated Warblers (both
very rare). Admittedly, warblers are the focus of most of the
Swan Point birders; however, thrushes, vireos, flycatchers,
and sparrows can be well worth looking for, too.

All of the eastern thrushes have occurred regularly here.
These include Veery, Hermit Thrush, Wood Thrush, Swainson's Thrush, and Gray-cheeked Thrush (rarely detected).
One of the reasons why the Gray-cheeked Thrush is so uncommon in Rhode Island is that it is one of several species (others
are Olive-sided Flycatcher and Mourning Warbler) which
wait until conditions are optimal on their breeding grounds
before moving northward; therefore, when conditions are
right, these species fly north in a rush—and it seems that the
bulk of the population bypasses Rhode Island.

Flycatchers such as Least, Yellow-bellied, Alder, Acadian,

Willow, Great Crested, and Olive-sided can be found here during migration, as well as Eastern Phoebe, Eastern King-bird, and Eastern Wood-Pewee. The vireos, too, are a group that moves through the cemetery in respectable numbers; Solitary, Yellow-throated, Warbling, White-eyed, and Red-eyed (usually in that chronological order) can be found here as well as the rare Philadelphia Vireo (fall only).

Finally, the fields near Hawthorn Road and behind the maintenance building provide excellent habitat for rarer mi-grant sparrows such as Lincoln's, White-crowned, and occa-sionally Lark Sparrow.

Sometimes in the spring, strong southerly gales will push southern species out of their normal range and into the north-east. For example, Blue Grosbeak, Summer Tanager, and Kentucky Warbler are all species which show up in the north-east every year and have occurred at Swan Point Cemetery. Two rare warblers that you should look for are hybrids that result when Blue-winged Warblers cross with Golden-winged Warblers, which are very uncommon in Rhode Island.

Swan Point resounds with birds on an early May morning. The calls of such species as the Indigo Bunting, Blue-gray Gnatcatcher, Northern and Orchard Orioles, Eastern Wood-Pewee, Ruby-crowned Kinglet, and House Wren, along with the calls of the many migrant species, can be almost over-whelming at times.

In sharp contrast to the spring migration, the fall move-ment of land birds is not spectacular. This is partly because the fall migration is spread out over a few months, whereas spring migration is usually concentrated into the brief period be-tween mid-April and mid-May. We can assume that the num-ber of birds passing through is the same (if not more because of young birds), but they are just not noticed so easily. There is, however, one interesting hitch to the fall land bird migra-tion: certain species travel along the East Coast only in the fall. The two most notable species in the category are Connecticut Warbler and Philadelphia Vireo.

*Cape May
Warbler*

After the fall migration has tapered off, the wintering birds begin to buckle down to surviving the long winter ahead. Swan Point is often loaded with wintering American Robins, Northern Flickers, White-throated Sparrows, and Field Sparrows. The Red-bellied Woodpecker has been a regular winter visitor to this area for the past several years along with the tiny Winter Wren. Some other species which have made winter appearances are White-winged and Red Crossbills, Common Redpolls, and Evening Grosbeaks, and during the winter of 1978, Pine Grosbeaks were seen feeding on the fruits of the Hawthorns and Mulberries.

22

George B. Parker Woodland

▼

Specialties: Land Birds

S.***, Su.***, F.**, W.*

▼

The George B. Parker Woodland is a wonderful wildlife refuge owned and operated by the Audubon Society of Rhode Island. Of all of the Audubon refuges in the state that I have visited, Parker has the greatest abundance and diversity of wildlife. Many species of birds breed here and some of the less common ones can be very easy to find.

Parker is best birded in the spring, summer, and fall when most of the Neotropical migrants are visiting the state. And if you are an amateur botanist, Parker is a good place to see some interesting plants.

DIRECTIONS:

From the north, follow I-95 south to US 6 west (this exit is along the stretch of I-95 that runs through Providence). Follow US 6 west until it intersects RI 102; turn left onto RI 102 south and drive approximately 9.5 miles to Maple Valley Road on your left. Turn left onto this road and drive about 500 feet to the Parker Woodland parking lot on your left.

From the west, follow I-95 north to Exit 5B, "RI 102 north," and drive north on RI 102 for approximately 8.4 miles (1.7 miles past the RI 117 junction) to Maple Valley Road. Turn right onto this road and proceed as above.

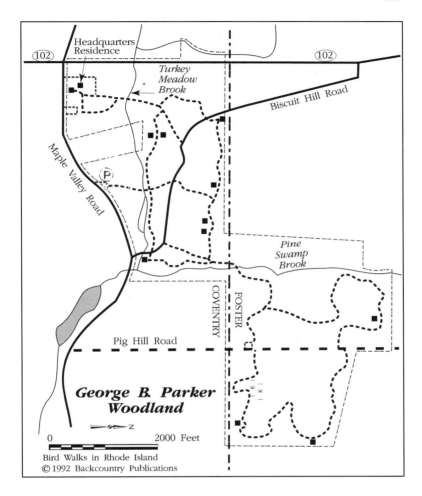

BIRDING:

Parker Woodland is a two-part refuge. The Coventry tract is the section for which directions are given. You can reach the Foster tract either by following the trails northward, or by following Maple Valley Road until you reach Pig Hill Road; turn left onto Pig Hill Road and walk this primitive and hilly one-lane road until you reach the Foster tract.

Parker Woodland is most notable for the Acadian Fly-catchers that breed here. Although there are only a few pairs, a walk through these woods in the spring or summer may reward you with a look at one of these small flycatchers. The best clue to this bird's presence and identification is its very distinctive "pit-see" call often heard echoing throughout the Beech stands of which they are so fond.

Other interesting species that breed at Parker are Worm-eating Warbler, which favors the rocky hillside cutcroppings; both the Northern and Louisiana Waterthrushes, the latter preferring to nest around the perennial woodland streams such as Turkey Meadow Brook and Pine Swamp Brook; and Yellow-throated Vireo, which can be easy to locate because of its very distinctive husky song. Cerulean Warblers were formerly found breeding here, so be sure to listen for them though they have not been seen in summertime at this refuge in several years.

Parker's trails provide relatively easy walking through a fine deciduous woodland. There are, however, some field and

Worm-Eating Warbler

The wooden bridge over Turkey Meadow Brook

wetland habitats as well as Pine groves, particularly near the refuge headquarters. Therefore, species that prefer these types of habitats are also found here; these include Field Sparrow, Chipping Sparrow, Prairie Warbler, Eastern Bluebird, Brown-headed Cowbird, and Tree Swallow.

Once you enter the woodland, though, you will see that the species composition will change dramatically. Northern Orioles, Rose-breasted Grosbeaks, Blue-gray Gnatcatchers, American Redstarts, Ovenbirds, Scarlet Tanagers, Blue-winged Warblers, Red-eyed Vireos, Eastern Wood-Pewees, and Great Crested Flycatchers will make their presence known to you throughout the summer by their characteristic songs and call notes.

During migration, Parker can also produce some interesting birds. Canada Warbler (breeds here), Solitary Vireo, Swainson's Thrush, and Blackburnian Warbler are all species to look for at this time.

While it is best to visit Parker during the spring and summer, winter birding can also be productive. If you can handle waking up at 4:30 A.M. to go owling, Parker is a fine place to do so. Entering this woodland at any trail and calling for owls will probably reward you with calls of at least one of the woodland owls: Great Horned, Barred (calls more frequently in spring than in winter), or Eastern Screech-Owl. These three species are all permanent residents at Parker.

23

Owling in Rhode Island

▼

Owls have always been somewhat of a mystery, partly because of most owls' nocturnal habits and partly because some people do not know how to go about finding owls. This section will be devoted entirely to helping birders find owls in the state of Rhode Island.

Most eastern owls, although not all, are nocturnal—that is, they are active only at night. It is unusual but not impossible to hear them calling during the daytime, but the best time to hear owls is just before sunrise. Owls can be heard calling year-round; however, you are most likely to get a response when the individual species is either setting up territory or tending to young—for example, from roughly January to May for the Great Horned Owl, and March to July for the Barred Owl.

Looking for owls can be a very enjoyable practice, and the thrill of hearing one in the distance or finding one in a day-roost is almost overwhelming. Owls are a difficult group to see, but do not become discouraged, for with a little patience and perseverance you will soon learn how to be in the right place at the right time and will be rewarded with owl sightings.

To call most owls, people use taped recordings of their songs. The best setup if you are going to make a tape is to have on tape several minutes of the desired species. (You can pick up recordings of bird songs from your Audubon Society.) Play this, and wait for a response. It is reasonably safe to say that if you have not heard a response after about 15 minutes, there are either no owls in the area or they simply do not wish to respond. Another method (much more fun) for calling owls is to imitate the calls yourself. Using various whistling and hooting techniques, you will learn that all of the owl calls are fairly easy to imitate—you will probably get a good laugh trying anyway.

Because of the months involved in the owling "season," it is best to dress warmly since the temperature can be very cold after midnight. Also, just as you might not go out on a night that is too cold for your taste, bear in mind that on unusually cold or windy nights most owls will not answer; it seems they too know when only a crazy person would be out.

I have broken down into separate categories all of the Rhode Island owls and provided as much information about their life history and best Rhode Island locality as is necessary to find them.

Great Horned Owl—Rhode Island's largest breeding owl. It prefers upland wooded areas where prey such as skunks and rabbits are abundant. Great Horned Owls begin nesting activities in January and are most often heard calling from January to May. They will respond readily to their own calls and occasionally to those of the Barred Owl. Buck Hill Management Area, Arcadia Management Area, and Parker Woodland are some of the better areas to look for this owl. Incidently, there is a pair of Great Horned Owls that breeds in Swan Point Cemetery every year; ask one of the local birders for the location—this is probably the easiest look at an owl you can get.

Barred Owl—the second largest breeding owl in the state. Barred Owls prefer wooded swamps much like those you will find at Great Swamp Management Area, Buck Hill Management Area, and Parker Woodland. The chief prey of this owl is smaller mammals, frogs, and other birds, particularly Screech-Owls if they are in the area. This owl will respond readily to its own species' calls and sometimes to those of the Great Horned Owl.

Eastern Screech-Owl—prefers drier woodlands and can often be rather common around cities and residential areas. This owl is usually the easiest to see since it responds readily to its call and usually flies in to investigate. However, many people will say that Screech-Owls will not call if they hear the calls of either the Great Horned Owl or the Barred Owl. The Eastern Screech-Owl feeds primarily upon small mammals and insects and can be found at locations such as Buck Hill Management Area, Parker Woodland, Trustom Pond, and any place where there are sufficient numbers of deciduous trees in which this little owl can find a roosting site.

Snowy Owl—the largest regularly occurring Rhode Island owl. Although Snowy Owls do not breed in the state, they are irruptive migrants; that is, they have sudden increases in number due to food fluctuations in the north. They therefore can, in some winters, be found easily. This owl perches conspicuously in coastal marshes and dunes which it prefers. Block Island, Sachuest Point, and Quonochontaug are the most likely places to see this owl if it is in the state at all.

Short-eared Owl—like the Snowy, strictly a winter visitor, preferring coastal areas with thick grass to hunt over and hide in. The Short-eared Owl is most often seen as it hunts (much like a Northern Harrier) low over the grass at dawn and dusk. Sachuest Point is by far the best and most reliable place in Rhode Island to find this owl.

Long-eared Owl—a very difficult species to find, although its breeding range includes Rhode Island. It prefers coniferous trees or thick Bittersweet tangles for roosting during the day. Most of the individuals seen in Rhode Island are probably wintering birds from the north. To look for these shy birds it is best to search Pine groves almost anywhere you can find them. Also, Long-eared Owls like to sun themselves in the early morning, so look for what appears to be a big, broken

Long-eared Owl

branch in the middle of a Bittersweet tangle and you may find your owl.

Barn Owl—prefers to nest in old barns or under cliff ledges, but spends the winter in large Pine groves. At favored roosting areas this owl can be regular. Block Island and the Norman Bird Sanctuary provide the most consistent sightings of this species.

Northern Saw-whet Owl—most often seen as a winter visitor. But there is considerable evidence to suggest that this tiny owl breeds very locally in the state. It should be searched for in the same Pine groves in which you would look for Long-eared Owls and Barn Owls. Saw-whet Owls are amazingly tame and will often allow very close approach once you have found one. Unfortunately, though, this tameness means that they will not reveal their presence by flushing, so luck and persistence are required to locate one.

24

Pelagic Birding

▼

Pelagic birds are birds that typically spend their entire lives out over the open ocean and only come ashore to breed; even then, most breed only on remote oceanic islands.

At the time of this writing there is not an easy way to see pelagic birds off the coast in Rhode Island. The F/V *Super Squirrel* out of Galilee harbor was the former means of transportation for local birders wishing to get out to Cox Ledge. However, this is no longer available.

You may be able to ride along as a bird-watcher on one of the other fishing boats leaving from Galilee harbor, but the current practice used by local captains is to charge bird-watchers full price (that is, the price you would pay if you were fishing) instead of half price as the *Super Squirrel* did. This cost may be prohibitive for some, as $50 or $60 is a terribly expensive way to spend an afternoon. Perhaps other more reasonable opportunities will become available. Contact the Rhode Island Audubon Society at (401) 231-6444 for up-to-date information on trips leaving from Rhode Island.

Fortunately, there are still other options available for pelagic birding. Regular whale-watching trips leave from Provincetown and Plymouth, Massachusetts. These trips, which can also be very good for bird-watching, usually go out to Stellwagon Bank, notable for the pelagic birds that can be seen there. For more information, call the Massachusetts Audubon Society at (617) 259-9500. To contact the whale-watching fleets directly, call (508) 255-3857 outside Massa-

Pomarine Jaeger

chusetts and 1-800-826-9300 inside Massachusetts for the
Dolphin Fleet which leaves from Provincetown; (508) 746-
2643 for the *Captain John* which leaves from Plymouth; (508)
283-0313 for the *Yankee Fleet* which leaves from Gloucester;
or (617) 973-5200 for the New England Aquarium boats
which depart from Boston. The cost of most of these trips is
about $15.

   Identifying pelagic birds can be difficult for many beginning birders, so to give you an idea of the types of species you
will probably encounter on your trip, I have structured this
chapter a bit differently. It is broken down by species and
includes key field marks to look for as well as the best times
of the year to find the various species. Pelagic birds tend to
wander widely, particularly nonbreeding birds and adults
after nesting. Therefore, a pelagic trip at any time may produce
some interesting results.

Greater Shearwater—seen chiefly during the summer months
(July–September). The North Atlantic is actually the winter
residence for this species as it breeds in the southern hemi-

sphere and disperses northward during the austral winter. The Greater Shearwater is fairly large (larger than a Great Black-backed Gull) with a dark bill. The dark-brown cap on the head contrasts markedly with the lighter-brown upperparts, the white neck-collar, and the largely white underparts. Also note the white band crossing the rump.

Cory's Shearwater—also seen chiefly during the summer months (July–September). Cory's is about the same size as the Greater Shearwater, but is longer winged, making it appear noticeably larger. The upperparts are uniformly gray-brown, contrasting less sharply with the white underparts, and the bill is mostly pale (a difficult character to see on the ocean). In general, Cory's looks like a large, unmarked, light-brown Shearwater.

Manx Shearwater—seen most often in summer and fall (June–October). Manx Shearwater is the smallest shearwater likely to be encountered. All-dark upperparts contrasting very sharply with the white underparts and white wing linings, along with rapid wing beats, distinguish this shearwater.

Sooty Shearwater—a summer visitor to the New England coast. Sooty is intermediate in size between Cory's and Manx Shearwaters. Except for silvery-white wing linings, it is entirely dark. It is the only all-dark eastern shearwater. Sooty is also the most abundant shearwater off the Rhode Island coast.

Wilson's Storm-Petrel—very common May–September. Look for the storm-petrel's very small size and almost swallow-like flight as it patters and hops across the waves to feed. It has all-dark plumage except for a white rump and undertail. Also note its short, relatively rounded wings and rounded or squarish tail. In fall plumage, it may have a distinct whitish bar on the upper wings.

Northern Fulmar—found chiefly in winter along the Rhode Island coast where it is uncommon to rare. The light-color phase predominates in the Atlantic (the dark-color phase in the Pacific). Look for a large gull-like bird flying on very stiff wings (the stiff-winged flight is the best field mark—you'll know it when you see it).

South Polar Skua—uncommon to rare; best chances are June–August. Looking like a very large, dark gull, it is a thick, heavy-set bird characterized by a pale buff collar on the hind neck and distinctive white bases to the primary feathers.

Pomarine Jaeger—seen occasionally during migration (May–July, August–September). Look for short, rounded and twisted tail-streamers; deep, regular falcon-like wing beats; and large, bulky size. White bases of the primary feathers are more extensive on the upper wing than on other jaegers.

Parasitic Jaeger—most frequently seen during fall migration (August–September). Parasitic Jaeger is smaller than the Pomarine Jaeger and has a more buoyant flight with faster wing beats. The tail-streamers are pointed, and the white at the primary bases is less extensive.

Other species which may be seen off the New England coast are Arctic Tern (seen rarely during migration), Northern Gannet (spring and fall), Black-legged Kittiwake (winter), and, occasionally offshore migrants such as Lesser Golden-Plover and Red and Red-necked Phalaropes. You may even see migrating warblers and other land birds that take refuge on the boat after being blown out to sea.

Rarities that have been seen in this area include Magnificent Frigatebird, Brown Pelican, Franklin's Gull, Audubon's Shearwater, Sabine's Gull, Long-tailed Jaeger, Leach's Storm Petrel, Great Skua, Red-billed Tropicbird, White-tailed Tropicbird, and Yellow-nosed Albatross.

25

Other Birding Areas

▼

This section provides general directions and information about birding for sixteen additional locations in the state. These areas all deserve mention but were not considered productive enough throughout the year to warrant greater treatment as a full chapter. However, for the species or seasons mentioned these are good areas. They are listed alphabetically.

Big River Management Area—Most of this management area is located in West Greenwich. The Big River area was recently saved from reservoir construction through the efforts of many private environmental organizations. This is fortunate because this area supports a number of interesting bird species. Pine Warblers, Solitary Vireos, Black-throated Green Warblers, Red-breasted Nuthatches, Purple Finches and Nashville Warblers are just a few of the species that breed here. I have listed two access points for this area although there are many others.

To reach this area follow I-95 south to exit 6A, "Hill Farm Road." If coming from the north, turn left at the end of the exit and follow this road for about .1 mile to the intersection with Division Road. Cross Division Road and continue for another .7 mile to a fork in the road. Bear right at this fork onto a dirt road and follow this road until you reach the gate. The trail starts behind the gate. Another access point can be reached by returning to Division Road and turning left. Follow this road for 1.8 miles to the RI 3 intersection. Turn left at this intersection onto RI 3 south and continue for 3 miles to Congdon Mill

Road at the traffic light on your left. Turn left onto this road for .8 mile to Burnt Sawmill Road (dirt road). Follow Burnt Sawmill Road for .4 mile to the gate. The trail starts behind the gate.

Charlestown Breachway—This breachway is one of the more common locations given on the Audubon Rare Bird Alert tape for finding migrating shorebirds and terns during the fall migration. Royal, Caspian, Roseate, and Black Terns are seen here regularly in the fall as well as Stilt Sandpiper, Baird's Sandpiper, and Long-billed Dowitcher.

To reach the breachway, follow US 1 in Charlestown to the "Cross Mills Pond, Charlestown Beach, Breachway" exit. Follow this exit to the first stop sign and turn left. Proceed .6 mile until you see a fork in the road at which point you will want to bear right. Follow this road .3 mile to "Charlestown Beach Road." Turn right onto this road and continue for another 1.3 miles until you reach another fork in the road. If you bear right at this fork and park in the parking lot, you will be at Charlestown Beach; if you bear left and follow this dirt road for .7 mile to its end you will be at the Charlestown Breachway, which is managed by the Rhode Island Department of Environmental Management. There is a fee charged at this area: Parking is $2 (resident) and $4 (nonresident). With your spotting scope, scan the sandbars in this area for the shorebirds and terns. Look thoroughly because there are numerous hidden mudflats where birds can be found.

Colt State Park—Colt State Park is located in Bristol and is a good place to see wintering Snow Buntings and Horned Larks. You should also check for wintering sea ducks in Narragansett Bay.

To reach this area, travel east on I-195 from Providence to the "RI 114 south" exit. Follow RI 114 south until you reach Bristol. Once in Bristol look for Asylum Road on your right. Turn right on this road and follow it to the park entrance.

Cross Mills Pond—Located in the southern part of the state in South Kingstown, Cross Mills Pond is most notable for the waterfowl that can be found here in the fall and winter. October, November, and December are the best months to find most waterfowl. Species to look for include Green- and Blue-winged Teals, Gadwall, Ring-necked Duck, and an occasional Redhead. Also look for Hooded and Common Mergansers as well as Pintail. With but one exception, the Blue-winged Teal, almost all of the freshwater waterfowl species can be found here throughout the winter, and if you visit frequently enough you should see most of them. This is also one of the better places in the state to see a fall Tundra Swan—November and December are good months to check.

You can reach this small pond by following US 1 south in South Kingstown to the first exit sign for RI 112 north. The pond is located just before the RI 112 exit and just past the first RI 112 exit sign on the US 1 south side. Park in the breakdown lane and beware of the heavy traffic.

Diamond Hill State Park—Located in the extreme northeast corner of the state (just south of Wrentham, Massachusetts), Diamond Hill State Park is a medium-sized park worth a look in the winter for Bald Eagles. Also check the reservoir for finches as well as wintering and migrating waterfowl and occasional white-winged gulls.

This park is located off RI 114 in Cumberland, Rhode Island and the reservoir can be found by heading east on Reservoir Road (just south of the park entrance).

Fish Road—This road is located in Tiverton and is one of the better places in the state to hear and sometimes see Hooded Warblers and Worm-eating Warblers.

To reach this area follow I-195 west from Providence to the Massachusetts exit 8A, "Tiverton, RI; Newport, RI." Follow this road (RI 24) south until you see the "Fish Road, Tiverton" exit. Turn left at the end of the exit and you are on

Fish Road. You can bird this area from the road or, the best way, you can go a few hundred yards up the road to the Rod and Gun Club and ask permission to walk their property.

Fogland Point and Fogland Marsh—Located in Tiverton, Fogland Point is a small park-like area where one can view the central and northern parts of the Sakonnet River. Look for terns during the summer, sea ducks during the winter, and shorebirds during the spring and fall migrations.

Fogland Marsh is a nice little marsh that is not frequented by birders although it very likely deserves to be visited often. In this marsh you will see migrating shorebirds and waders and maybe even an American Bittern. Also, look for American Oystercatchers. At least one pair probably breeds here.

To reach this area, travel south on RI 77 4.4 miles from the RI 177 intersection to Pond Bridge Road on the right. Turn right onto this road and proceed .3 mile to a fork. Bear right at the fork and this will take you directly to the dirt parking lot at the tip of Fogland Point. To reach the Fogland Marsh, bear left at the fork mentioned above and follow this road as it winds to the right until you see the beach. Park along the road in front of the beach and walk east along the beach for about 150 yards. If you look over the small dune to the north you will see the marsh.

Green Hill Pond—Located in South Kingstown, this pond can be a good shorebird spot during the fall migration. Several years ago a Black Rail was reported to have been calling from this marsh.

To reach Green Hill Pond follow US 1 south in South Kingstown to the Moonstone Beach exit. Follow Moonstone Beach Road south until you reach Matunuck Schoolhouse Road. At this road turn right and follow it until you reach Green Hill Beach Road. Turn left onto this road and follow it to the end. From several locations you can get a view of the pond and the birds that can be found here.

Hundred Acre Cove—Located in Barrington along the Barrington River, Hundred Acre Cove is an excellent spot to look for waterfowl in winter as well as Sharp-tailed and Seaside Sparrows in the summer.

To reach this cove follow I-195 east from Providence to the RI 114 south exit. Follow RI 114 south for a couple of miles until you see the first large cove on your left.

Long Pond and Ell Pond—Located in the western part of the state in Hopkinton, Long Pond and Ell Pond provide a wonderful area to walk through and to see birds such as Hooded Warblers, Worm-eating Warblers, and migrant land birds in the spring and fall.

To reach this area from the east follow RI 138 west from the University of Rhode Island in Kingston to the junction of RI 3 north and RI 138. Continue on RI 138 west past this junction for .8 mile until you see a sign for RI 138 west. Follow

Northern Shoveler and Mallard

RI 138 west from this point for 2.7 miles to Wincheck Pond Road. Turn left onto this road and proceed .1 mile to Canochet Road on your left. Turn left here and follow this road for .4 mile until you see a fork in the road; bear right onto an unmarked road. This road becomes dirt after .5 mile. Drive for another .5 mile to a small pull-off parking area on your left. Park here to pick up the Yellow Trail.

Lonsdale Marshes—Located just north of Providence in Lincoln, the Lonsdale Marshes can be a very productive spot for migrating land birds in the spring. There is a dirt road and several trails off this road which you can walk to find Warbling Vireos, Nashville Warblers, and Marsh Wrens. The marshes here are one of the best places in the state to see Virginia Rails and Sora Rails. If you play a recorded tape of their calls, they will often answer you and sometimes a Virginia Rail will walk directly in front of you or come up and do everything but peck at your shoe.

To reach the marshes, travel east on RI 123 from the back parking lot of Lincoln Woods State Park for 1 mile to RI 122 (Lonsdale Avenue). Turn right onto RI 122 and proceed .3 mile until you see the gate on your left. Sometimes the gate is open and you can park near the softball field. If the gate is not open, I would suggest parking on the unimproved road on the other side. This section of RI 122 is dangerous. Oncoming cars may have trouble seeing you. So be very careful parking and crossing the road!

Ministerial Road—Known also as RI 110, this road is located between US 1 along the south shore and RI 138 in Kingstown. Birds of particular interest that can be found here along the trail located off RI 110 are breeding Hooded Warblers, Worm-eating Warblers, Canada Warblers, and Northern Waterthrushes. This trail is worth a hike during the spring and fall migrations for land birds.

To reach this trail along Ministerial Road, travel 1.3 miles south on RI 110 from the RI 138 intersection to the trail on your left. From the south, travel 3.6 miles north on RI 110 from the US 1 junction to the trail on your right. Look for a small turnoff from the road and you will see the gate that marks the beginning of this trail.

Quonset Point—Located in North Kingstown, Quonset State Airport is one of the last places in the state where you can find Upland Sandpipers and Grasshopper Sparrows. Also look for Eastern Meadowlarks, Bobolinks, and Savannah Sparrows.

To reach this area, follow US 1 south in North Kingstown to the entrance to Davisville and Quonset Point. Turn left at this entrance and after .1 mile turn right at the Seabee statue. At the traffic light about .2 mile down the road, bear left. Follow this road for about .7 mile until you see the sign "NCBC Housing and Retrieving" on your right. Turn right here and follow this road straight for .2 mile to a fence gate. If the gate is open, continue on to the next gate which is always closed and look for the birds on your right in the field (it is best if you can use a spotting scope for this). Often the first gate is closed; if so, you can walk around the right side of it.

Ram Tail Road and Ponagansett Road—Although unimproved, these roads provide some of the best spring birding in the state. In May you should drive them slowly and listen for migrating warblers such as Cerulean, Mourning, and Wilson's Warblers, not to mention the abundant species such as American Redstarts and Blue-winged Warblers. Also, Ruffed Grouse can be heard drumming in early May. I didn't say "listen" for Ruffed Grouse, because I don't think you actually hear them but rather you feel the sound in your ears. Go to this area and you will know what I am talking about.

To reach Ram Tail Road and Ponagansett Road, you should travel west on US 6 (be sure to follow the signs for US 6 and stay on it) from the RI 116 junction in Scituate. Heading west from this junction, drive 5.9 miles until you see a sign for Round Hill Road on your left. Turn left here because Round Hill Road is also good for birding. Follow Round Hill Road for 1.1 miles until you come to a small intersection—cross the road here and you will be on Ponagansett Road. Ponagansett Road is 2 miles to its end. Ram Tail Road is 1 mile past Round Hill Road on US 6. The sign for this road can only be seen from the other direction, so look for a cemetery on the left and turn left here. Ram Tail Road is 1.3 miles long. Bird these roads slowly, either on foot or in a car, because this area can be extremely productive.

Richmond Turf Farms—Located between the Great Swamp Management Area and the Carolina Management Area, the Richmond Turf Farms are an excellent place to find migrating shorebirds in the spring and fall. Usually after heavy rains low spots in the turf become saturated, and this provides ideal foraging areas for Least, White-rumped, Pectoral, Buff-breasted, and occasional Upland Sandpipers. Lesser Golden Plovers can sometimes be found here in the fall as well as Common Snipe, Stilt Sandpiper, and both yellowlegs species. The trick is to find which area has been recently watered or is accumulating rain water. Do not walk on the turf grass. Make your observations from the paved roads. Farm owners can become very irritated if you are trespassing on their property. Occasionally they will allow you to walk along the dirt roads that crisscross their farms, but only if you ask permission.

The Richmond Turf Farms can be reached by driving toward the University of Rhode Island in Kingston from either the north or the west. The best areas to check are located just south of the campus on RI 2.

Trestle Trail—Located in Coventry, Trestle Trail provides the opportunity to see good land birds during the spring and fall migrations. One species seen here with fair regularity in the fall is the Philadelphia Vireo. Other interesting species seen during migration are Blackpoll Warblers and Swainson's Thrushes. Also, Warbling Vireos, Yellow Warblers, Eastern Phoebes, and Willow Flycatchers can be found breeding along the wetter areas of this trail.

To reach the easiest access point for this trail, you should drive east on RI 117 from the RI 102 junction for 3.7 miles to Hill Farm Road on your right. Turn right onto Hill Farm Road and follow it for .1 mile to the dirt parking area on your right. The trail starts behind the large cement boulders. Dirt-bikers and fishermen are common in this area, but good birds are too, so do not be discouraged if you see hordes of people. Although this trail continues all the way to the Connecticut border, the first three miles usually provide the best birding.

Wood River Junction—This area is located in Richmond and is a good place to see early migrant Tree Swallows and Eastern Phoebes as well as migrating waterfowl.

To reach this area drive west from the University of Rhode Island in Kingston on RI 138 until you reach the RI 112 south intersection. Go south on RI 112 until you reach RI 91 south. Turn onto RI 91 south until you reach the intersection of RI 91 and Hope Valley Road. You will see a large lake on the right—this is the place to stop and look for birds.

Bibliography

▼

Bowen, Richard. *Nesting Birds of Block Island* (Block Island Conservancy and the Audubon Society of Rhode Island, 1981)

Conway, Robert A. *Field Checklist of Rhode Island Birds* (Providence, RI: Audubon Society of Rhode Island, 1979)

Emerson, David, ed. *Field Notes of Rhode Island Birds*, Numbers 201–238 (1985–88). (Smithfield, RI: Rhode Island Ornithological Club and the Audubon Society of Rhode Island)

Ferren, Richard L. *The Birds of the East Providence Reservoir* (Providence, RI: Audubon Society of Rhode Island)

Fry, Adam. *Comprehensive List of the Birds of Rhode Island, 1900–1989* (Smithfield, RI: Rhode Island Ornithological Club / Audubon Society of Rhode Island, 1990)

Weber, Ken. *More Walks and Rambles in Rhode Island* (Woodstock, VT: Backcountry Publications, 1992)

Weber, Ken. *Walks and Rambles in Rhode Island* (Woodstock, VT: Backcountry Publications, 1988)

Wood, Charles. *The Birds of Swan Point Cemetery* (Providence, RI: Proprietors of Swan Point Cemetery, 1981)

Index

▼

Also from The Countryman Press and Backcountry Publications

The Countryman Press and Backcountry Publications, long known for fine books on nature, outdoor recreation, and travel offer a range of practical and readable manuals.

Other Books on Birds and Nature

Backyard Bird Habitat, by Will and Jane Curtis, $9.95
Earthmagic: Finding and Using Medicinal Herbs,
　by Corinne Martin, $14.95
*Our Native Fishes: The Aquarium Hobbyist's Guide to Observing,
　Collecting and Keeping Them*, by John Quinn, $14.95

Books on Rhode Island and neighboring states

Canoeing Massachusetts, Rhode Island, and Connecticut,
　by Ken Weber, $9.95
Fifty Hikes in Connecticut, by Gerry and Sue Hardy, $11.95
Fifty Hikes in Massachusetts, by John Brady and Brian White, $12.95
More Walks and Rambles in Rhode Island, by Ken Weber, $9.95
Newport, Rhode Island: A Guide to the City by the Sea,
　by Tom Gannon, $11.95
25 Mountain Bike Tours in Massachusetts, by Robert S. Morse, $9.95
Walks and Rambles in Rhode Island, by Ken Weber, $9.95
Walks and Rambles on Cape Cod and the Islands, by Ned Friary
　and Glenda Bendure, $10.95

Other Travel Books on New England and the Northeast

Family Resorts of the Northeast, by Nancy Pappas Metcalf, $12.95
Maine: An Explorer's Guide, by Christina Tree
　and Mimi Steadman, $16.95
New England's Special Places, by Michael Schuman, $12.95
New Hampshire: An Explorer's Guide, by Christina Tree
　and Peter Randall, $16.95
Vermont: An Explorer's Guide, by Christina Tree
　and Peter Jennison, $16.95

We offer many more books on hiking, walking, fishing, canoeing, and cross-country skiing in New England, New York State, the Mid-Atlantic states, and the Midwest—plus books on travel, nature, gardening, and many other subjects.

Our titles are available in bookshops and in many sporting goods stores, or they may be ordered directly from the publisher. When ordering by mail, please add $2.50 per order for shipping and handling. To order or obtain a complete catalog, please write The Countryman Press, Inc., P.O. Box 175, Woodstock, Vermont 05091.